BEING
A PROACTIVE
GRANDFATHER

#1GPA

FAMILIUS

Library of Congress Cataloging-in-Publication Data
2017941438

Print ISBN 9781945547270
Ebook ISBN 9781945547621

Printed in the United States of America

Edited by Lindsay Sandberg
Cover design by David Miles
Book design by Brooke Jorden

10 9 8 7 6 5 4 3 2 1

First Edition

BEING
A PROACTIVE
GRANDFATHER

HOW TO MAKE A
DIFFERENCE

NEW YORK TIMES #1 BESTSELLING AUTHOR
RICHARD EYRE

I would like to dedicate this book to a whole generation of men—the generation we call Baby Boomers (forty million of us in the United States) who are all, now, as this book is published, in our fifties or sixties or very early seventies. We are the biggest generation ever and the first in history to have an extra decade or two to play around with, or to continue working with, or to devote to our families and our relationships. May we all choose well!

I also want to dedicate this book to Linda, my wife and partner of forty-seven years, a.k.a. Grammie, who is so excellent in that role (and so joyful in it) that she shamed/loved me into trying harder and doing better in my counterpoint role.

MEN OF A CERTAIN AGE

There're a lot of us,
Guys between fifty-five and seventy-five,
Wondering
What to do next.
Still plenty of energy and more capacity
Than ever before,
At the peak of our powers.
So what?
Keep working until we die, extend the routine?
Retire, find a house on a golf course, pull back, dry up?
Travel, leave everyone and everything behind?
Start a new career, start over, and take risk?
What if we want a little of all these,
But we want something more?
For most of us, there is another option,
For our effort and energy, our focus and force,
Hidden in plain sight, right under our noses:
Grandkids!
Little extensions of ourselves, legacies,
Growing up in a world that is harder
And more complex
Than ours was, or our kids' was.
They need us,
And we need them—there can be symbiosis.
We know there is delight there, and opportunity,
But we don't know how, or when, or even what;
We're not confident as Grandfathers and
Our role is not clear.
That's the reason for this book.

You may have noticed that the first BIG word in this book's title is BEING.

That is because this is less a book about *doing* than about *becoming*.

Being an exceptional grandfather is not about changing your grandkids.

It is about changing yourself.

It is about *being* the kind of grandfather your grandkids need.

The second BIG word in the title is GRAND.

What does the "grand" mean in grandfather?

Well, technically, from the etymology dictionary, *Grand* means "one generation removed in ascent."

I didn't love that definition, so I looked up "grand" in the regular dictionary and found something much better:

"Magnificent or splendid."

And the second definition wasn't bad either:

"Noble or revered."

It is well to remember, of course, that
Your grandkids are not my grandkids;

My family situation is not your family situation,
Your financial and personal circumstances
Are not my circumstances;
My life is not your life, and yours is not mine.
Each of us is unique.
So it is not likely (or prudent) that you will copy
Or replicate
My suggestions
Or try to clone what I am trying to become
As a grandfather.
That's not the point.
The point (and the goal) is that
We all think about this stage of life,
That we share ideas and perspectives,
And that each of us comes up with
Our personal and unique
Strategy for BEING GRANDfathers.

Once again, keep in mind that this is not a book about grandkids or what you want to make of them or turn them into; it is a book about grandfathering—about what you want to be—about the kind of granddad you want to become.

Since you don't have to be a disciplinarian or a friend-monitor or a taxi driver or an agenda-maker and scheduler or an allowance-giver or a feeder and clothier like you were as a dad, you can now choose other roles to play as a granddad—fun roles, joyous roles, difference-making roles, roles that can help your grandkids make good decisions, find their gifts, fulfill their potential, and transform their confidence and identity.

There are ten things I want to do for my grandchildren—ten gifts I want to give them; ten blessings that I am perfectly positioned and uniquely qualified to deliver; ten things I want to *be* for them; ten roles I want to play in their lives; ten things I believe I can become for them if I work hard enough at each of them . . .

And those ten things are the ten chapters of this book.

Contents

One who connects with them individually and who becomes the master of active listening

One who gives confidence, self-worth, and an appreciation for who they really are—and who they can become

One who understands that parents are the coaches and kids are the stars, but who can step in to play specific needed roles and to fill in when there are voids

One who connects grandkids to their ancestors and shares a family narrative that can build their larger identity and ensure their resilience

One who listens and lifts and helps them set and reach their own goals

One who works out ways for them to earn things for themselves and who substitutes grit for entitlement

One who teaches the principles that really matter in an exclusive, exciting, and secretive way

One who brings everyone together for reunions, creating fun times, bonding, loyalty, and lasting friendships between cousins

One who provides the matching grants, loans, and equity that can fuel grandkids' initiative and help them move forward faster toward their goals

One who awakens them to their own options and potential and to the diversity of the world

■ GRANDPARENTING □
QUESTION:

CAN GRANDFATHERS SAVE THE WORLD?

B asically, I believe that granddads can save the world—and have a lot of fun doing it. (Grandmas, too, but that's another book because the two roles are different and distinct.)

When we ask, "Who is going to teach this generation of children the values, the character, the family narrative, even the street smarts that they will need?" most would say that the ideal answer is "the parents." But in today's world, where most parents work full time, and where life's options and challenges seem to be increasing exponentially, who is to say that parents will find the time or the means?

So who else can possibly do it? Grandfathers!

Who will give kids the confidence, the identity, and maybe even the resources they need to become all they can be? Same ideal answer, but the same problem. So the same saving answer: grandparents!

There can be an incredible connection, even a symbiosis, between generations one and three. It is a connection that can preserve traditions, that can build character, and that can bring joy to both sides.

And it's not a new connection, not by any means. Most of the world works like this—grandparents doing much of the teaching, nurturing, identity building, and supporting, while the parents are earning the living. Three-generation households are the norm and not the exception everywhere but in the richest countries. And the kids and the grandparents are the happier for it.

We don't need to live in the same house with them, but we grandpas can save the world by how proactively we GRANDfather our grandchildren. The purpose of this book is to help a little with the "hows."

Let's think this through together.

Four Man-to-Man Grandfathering Options

This is a man-to-man book. As a Baby Boomer man with kids and grandkids, I'm writing to other Baby Boomer men with kids and grandkids. I write as a man with a lot of interests, passions, and priorities, and I write to other men who also have a lot of interests, passions, and priorities. We have our careers; we have our sports and our friends and our hobbies and our travel and our music and our other personal interests; we have our finances and our investments; we have our causes, our bucket lists, our cars, our boats, and our toys;

we have our politics and our clubs and our churches and our other responsibilities. We have our siblings and our extended families, and some of us still have our own aging parents. And we have our children, who, even as adults, are still our children.

But none of us, when we really sit down and think about it, have anything quite as delightful and as joyful as our grandchildren. They are our flesh and blood. They are our pride and joy. And ultimately, they are our only real legacy.

How much of our time and our mental energy are we devoting to those precious and perfect little kids who carry our name and our genetics and our view of the world? And how deliberate and thoughtful are we about the time we spend with them, about what we can do for them, about the relationship we want with them now and for the rest of our lives?

How grand is grandfathering? About as grand as you make it!

We don't get a lot of training about how to be grandfathers. There is no owner's guide or instruction manual. (This book may be the closest thing you can get.)

When your kids have kids, you have a decision to make: What kind of grandfather will you be? And if you've been a granddad for a while now, but not yet made that decision, now might be the time to make it.

There are several alternatives, and each comes with a different attitude:

1. Disengaged Grandfathering.

Attitude: I raised my kids and now it's their turn to raise their kids; I'm done.

This attitude might lead you to downsize into an adults-only condo in Sun City by a golf course, where your days would be quiet, but boring.

2. Limited Grandfathering.

Attitude: I love to see them but in limited doses and on my terms.

In this model, grandkids are like amusement parks; you go there once in a while to have fun. Or like dinner guests; you have them over now and then, when it's convenient.

3. Supportive Grandfathering.

Attitude: My kids need all the help they can get with their kids, and I want to be there for them.

With this approach, you become part helper, part martyr, sacrificing your own life to be at the beck and call of your adult children whenever they "need" you to help with kids.

4. Proactive Grandfathering.

Attitude: My children are the stewards for their children, but I can teach these grandkids things their parents can't and be an essential part of an organized, three-generation family. And by thinking about it—hard—and coming up with a strategy and a plan, I can make a real difference in my grandkids' lives, even as I add joy to my own life and keep myself young.

Only at this fourth level does grandfathering become effective, consequential, and truly fun. At this level, you deliberately ponder the needs you can uniquely fulfill and you set goals and plans to enhance your grandchildren's lives; and you do so in concert and in teamwork with the goals and stewardship of their parents. This approach will stretch and test you, but it will also reward you with levels of fulfillment, well-being, love, and peace otherwise unobtainable.

Let's use this book to explore the possibilities. And let's do it not only in terms of everything you might *do* for your grandkids, but in the more consequential and controllable terms of what you can *be* for and to your grandkids. I'll say it again: being an effective, influential grandfather is not about changing the grandkids; it's about changing yourself!

If you are just looking for a couple of quick tips or quick fixes, this is probably not the right book. But if you are looking to truly prioritize your grandchildren and to be the kind of champion, companion, and senior consultant that they need, read on!

Richard Eyre
Park City, Utah
Fall 2017

THE JOY AND THE MIRACLE OF GRANDKIDS

N ow that I've tried to narrow the readership down to men willing to accept the challenge of Proactive Grandfathering, I can begin to speak more candidly and unapologetically about accepting the role with gusto and making a difference.

Let's think about legacy for a moment: Which would you rather have, a bridge named after you or grandchildren who carry on your name and genetics, and live noble, contributing lives that make you proud? At our age, we should be putting our time and energy into things that can really make a difference—things that will make up our legacy. And those things are not really *things* at all; they are our grandchildren.

The fact is that we can and should play a powerful role in teaching our grandchildren to live for responsibility and reputation, rather than ease and entitlement. And we should realize by now that, in the end, it all boils down to family.

After an event with a group of terrific proactive parents in Aspen, Colorado, last year, I sat with the organizer of the event and his wife for a little private consultation at dinner. Their biggest question had nothing to do with anything I had talked about during my presentation. Their main personal concern was that their fathers didn't know their children. The two granddads, having worked hard to raise their own children, had apparently decided that their job was done. It was time for them to do what they wanted to do—to retire in a sunny place and play golf and let their kids deal with their children on their own.

This young couple had three beautiful children, and they were desperate for their fathers to be a part of those children's lives. The two grandmas were fully vested and engaged, but not the granddads. These parents felt that not only were the kids losing out on knowing what great people their grandfathers were, but that the granddads were missing an opportunity to be champions for their grandchildren. The couple had mentioned that their oldest son, a teenager, was struggling with several issues and that their communication with him had become strained and difficult. They felt that the boy would listen to one of his granddads if either of them would just take more of an interest.

I suggested that they call or meet with their fathers and

explain the situation with the teenager and ask for their advice and help as a beginning step in helping those two dads get more vested and involved with their grandkids. I felt sad thinking about the good things this family was missing by not having their dads involved in their kids' lives!

Thankfully, although there are plenty of granddads like the ones in this story, it is not the norm. The norm is to want to be involved, helpful, focused, and effective as grandfathers. But the norm is also not to know quite *how* to do it.

Surveys show that 72 percent of Baby Boomer dads who have grandchildren think being a grandparent is the single most important and satisfying thing in their life.[1] But thinking that and knowing what to do about it are two different things.

As we reach retirement age, we are the first generation in history with an average of another good twenty to thirty years of life ahead of us. So, more than any other granddads of any other time, we ought to be committed to being proactive grandfathers.

It is an important enough thing to deserve a strategy—a plan. This book is about formulating that plan and tailoring it to your own unique situation and your own unique family.

Parts of this book's content are taken from a longer book I wrote with my wife, Linda, called *Life in Full*, which tries to develop an overall formula or approach for making the "autumn" of our lives the best and the fullest season. The

---

1. "Surprising Facts About Grandparents." *Grandparents.com*. http://www.grandparents.com/food-and-leisure/did-you-know/ surprising-facts-about-grandparents

center core of that formula is to become a truly involved and proactive grandparent. This book is an elaboration and an expansion of that theme, and it's aimed at the granddad side of the formula, since most grandmas seem to do it all a little more instinctively.

Linda and I were speaking on a cruise ship to 150 "seniors," and we asked how many of them would want to go back and be twenty or thirty again. Two hands went up. The rest said no. When we asked why, they said, essentially, that life is better now. When we asked why again, the predominate answer was "grandkids!"

Ahhhh, grandkids. There is nothing like them. Mary H. Waldrip said, "Grandchildren are God's way of compensating us for growing older." Joan McIntosh said, "They say genes skip generations. Maybe that's why grandparents find their grandchildren so likeable."

It's not that grandkids are easy, physically or any other way. As Gene Perret put it, "My grandkids believe I'm the oldest thing in the world. And after two or three hours with them, I believe it, too." And an unknown author, speaking realistically, said, "I have a warm feeling after playing with my grandchildren. It's the liniment working."

There is an old Welsh proverb that says, "Perfect love sometimes does not come until the first grandchild." And Alex Haley said, "Nobody can do for little children what grandparents do. Grandparents sort of sprinkle stardust over the lives of little children."

Let's work on it together!

■ GRANDPARENTING ▢
CHAPTER 1

BEING THEIR
ONE-ON-ONE FRIEND

ONE WHO CONNECTS WITH THEM INDIVIDUALLY
AND WHO BECOMES THE MASTER
OF ACTIVE LISTENING

WHAT DO THEY CALL YOU AND WHAT DO YOU CALL THEM?

I t is amazing how many names there are for granddads! Some of them make no sense at all, yet are individualistic and endearing. Others are logical. Still others are, well, sort of weird. We know a family who calls the grandfather "Poobah," and another who calls their guy "Stinky." (I'd like to know the story behind that one.) We know grandkids with Swedish ancestry who call one of their grandfathers "Morfar" and the other one "Farfar." (In Swedish, *Morfar* means mother's father and *Farfar* means father's father.)

The most common names seem to be Grandpa and Granddad, but there are a lot of variations like Grandpop and Papa and Granddaddy and Granddada.

In my case—and this takes some explaining, lest you think me overly formal or authority seeking—my grandkids call me by the original and proper name, Grandfather. As with so many granddad names, it wasn't chosen or planned; it came about circumstantially. The first grandson, learning to talk, was sitting with his mother one day when I walked in. My daughter said, "Look, it's your grandfather."

"Gamfadder?" the little guy said, and it sounded so cute that it stuck, and when he outgrew his baby talk it became "Grandfather." The humorous advantage of having that for my name is that none of the new grandchildren, as they come along, can pronounce it; and as each tries, new variations come along for our entertainment: "GaFa," "Gamfa,"

"Gafad," "Fadder," "Dodder," all gradually morph into the name I now love, Grandfather.

So, maybe it was a natural progression that I started feeling, fairly early on, that if they each, in their babyhood, had a unique name for me, I should have a unique name just for them—something that no one else called them that sort of set our relationship apart as something unique. Like their names for me, they weren't planned or thought out, they just kind of evolved. I started calling our first grandson, whose name is Maxwell, "Maximilian," which got shortened to "Million," and I shortened our oldest granddaughter, Elle, to "L." I now have my own name for each of them, and they like it. Recently, as we were on our way to visit our little five-year-old granddaughter, Annina, her dad called as they awaited our arrival, and he said that Annina had just said to him, "I miss Grandfather—he's the only one who calls me NeNe."

This is all to illustrate the notion that we all need to have a unique and individual relationship with our grandchildren. Whether we have one of them or twenty of them, each one deserves to feel how special and individual he or she is in our eyes.

GET TO KNOW THEM ONE-ON-ONE AND DO "GRANDFATHER DATES"

It is amazing how many grandfathers have spent virtually no time with their grandchildren one-on-one or in situations where the parents are not present. Kids are different in environments where parents are not with them. It brings out other aspects of their personalities, and you see them in a different light. We grandfathers need to volunteer to babysit, occasionally, where it is just us and the kids, and find other ways to get to know them by themselves, without parents around.

In fact, we should make it our conscious goal to get to know each grandchild one-on-one—to really know them and to keep updating what you know about them as they grow older. Get in the habit of going on individual "Grandfather Dates"—usually to eat—and let them pick the restaurant. Take along an impressive-looking notebook or "grandpa datebook," ask them questions, and take notes on their answers. Tell them you want to know as much as you can about them, so you can always be their cheerleader and their helper. Ask them everything from their favorite color and food to what they think they might be when they grow up. Hand them the pen and let them fill in some things in your notebook like, "The three words that best describe me are . . ." or "The best thing and the worst thing in my life right now is . . ."

Don't editorialize too much during these date discussions. Just ask a lot of questions and listen. And take notes.

Use the great word "really" to keep them talking. You can say "really" so many ways and in so many contexts. "Really!" as in "Wow!" "Really" as in "Whoa, I never knew that." "Really?" as in "Are you serious?" "Really!?" as in "What the heck!" With the appropriate inflection, that one word can keep kids talking and connecting.

Have them make a list in your notebook of "things I am sure I will do in my life," and "things I might do in my life," and "things I will never do in my life." When I asked that last question to my ten-year-old granddaughter on our date, hoping for something like "I will never do drugs," she thought for a moment and said, "I will never ride a bike naked in public!" I said, "Really!?" and she said, "When we were in San Francisco, we saw this guy ride by naked and I said to myself right then, 'I will never do that!'"

As your grandkids get into their mid- and late-teens, you want to transition into their consultants and their non-judgmental advisors, and maybe their financial supporters for education and other worthwhile pursuits; those earlier Grandfather Dates will set the stage for that.

Tell them what a consultant is and tell them that your door or your computer or your phone is always open to them and that you will always LOVE it when they ask for help or for advice of any kind. Tell them you know their parents are always first, but you are the backup. And tell them you want to know everything you can about them, because the more you know, the more helpful you can be.

If you don't live close enough to your grandkids to have regular Grandfather Dates, carve out some special, individual time when you are visiting their family or they are visiting you. And in the "between times," get on Skype or FaceTime with them one-on-one.

Social Media, Personal Letters, and "Private Clubs"

Essential to communication with any grandkids, whether they live far away or just down the street, is your own competence and confidence with social media.

I used to use email, but we have found that our older grandchildren and teenagers never look at their email accounts, even if they have them. They do use Facebook and Twitter and Instagram and Snapchat. As we will discuss later in the book, keeping up with their technology is indispensable in our ongoing ability to communicate with our grandkids.

Especially fun for the little preschoolers is FaceTime and Skype. It's such a simple way to keep up with what is going on with your long-distance grandchildren! And, by the way, if you don't have a clue how to use these sites or apps, just let your grandkids help you.

I've had some of our most delightful interchanges with our grandchildren through our current personal favorite— Instagram. Just commenting on their posts lets them know that I am aware of what they are doing. It may also make them a little more aware of what they post and give a second thought to posting anything that may be inappropriate.

And while you are going high-tech, go low-tech too by writing your grandchild something he or she may have never seen or received before: an actual stamped, sealed, handwritten letter. I write an "unbirthday" letter to each of my grandchildren on their half-birthday. I do it on real stationery with a fountain pen. I tell them what I love about them, and I send the letters by the US mail!

Beyond just being in touch and communicating liberally with grandkids, we ought to have an intimate and exclusive relationship with each grandkid based on his or her current interests and whatever intrigues him or her at the moment.

I have a separate two-member "club" with each grandchild. The nature of each club is based on the predominate passion of that grandchild. For example, nine-year-old Charlie and I have the "Baseball Club," and one of the main things we do is try to stump each other on obscure baseball terms. He recently stumped me on "Texas Leaguer." (I had forgotten that it meant a pop fly that was just over the infielder that dropped in for a hit.) But I got him on "Chin music," which he didn't know referred to a brush back pitch thrown inside to move the batter back off the plate.

Each grandchild is different. But through learning about their individual interests and communicating with them individually, we can find a way to let each know that they are our favorite!

GIVE EACH GRANDCHILD A JOURNAL AND A CHALLENGE TO MAKE "DECISIONS IN ADVANCE"

An effective way to get to know kids individually, in terms of their future as well as their present and past, is to give each of them a powerful gift I've called, "The decisions in advance diary." This can be a powerful molder of your grandchildren's character, and you can be their mentor in this classic way of avoiding bad choices and resisting peer pressure.

It's a fairly simple process, and a good way to get it started is to buy a very special journal as a gift on each child's eighth birthday (or if you have older grandkids, just give the gift now). If they are already in the diary or journal-writing habit, just make this the best new journal they have ever had. Get a leather one or another type that is very nice and very permanent—it's worth the money. If your grandchild is not journaling, encourage it and tell him about the benefits of keeping track of his life.

In either case, tell your recipient grandchild that you want him or her to reserve the back few pages of the journal for "Decisions in Advance."

Ask what decisions they think they could make right now, even though they have not yet faced those decisions. Explain that the worst time to make decisions is in the moment, when there will be peer pressure and when it is hard to think clearly.

Have a little fun in your explanation by asking "obvious" questions like, "Can you decide right now who you are going to marry?" "Can you decide in advance what your career is going to be?" "Can you choose right now where you are going to live when you are thirty?" Of course not. But could you decide right now, if you wanted to, that you were not going to smoke? Or try drugs? Or ride in a car with a driver who has been drinking? Or shoplift? Or cheat on tests? Can you decide in advance whether or not you will go to college? Whether or not you will help a kid who is being bullied?

Explain that the list of "Decisions in Advance" in their journal is only for things they feel sure they have decided. In your discussions, when they think they have made a certain decision in advance, give them a case study or two about how hard it might be and how much pressure they might feel from friends. When they (and you) feel that the decision in advance is strong and real, have them write it on their list, date it, and sign it with their signature. Tell them that you are there for them and that you want to be their advisor and consultant on things like this and that you will come back and talk about their list often.

SUMMARY AND GUIDELINES

Some say it this way: "You want each grandchild to be convinced that he or she is your favorite." Whether you like that phrase or not, we would probably all agree that we want individual, personal, and unique relationships with each of our grandchildren. Review some of the approaches that lead to that kind of bond:

> » *Have your own name and your own club for and with each grandchild.* Have a private nickname for each grandchild that makes him or her feel individual and special and start a special two-member club centered on what each of them loves most.
> » *Take them on Grandfather Dates to places they choose to go and keep a notebook of their answers to the questions you ask them.* Become the master of the probing questions and take notes so you can

pick up and update during the next date you have
with them.

» *Use the social media they use and have them tutor
you on how it works.* "Meet them where they are"
electronically and make the effort to be social-media
savvy and to get a consistent back and forth going
with each grandchild.

» *Know their specific and individual interests and be
involved.* And stay up to date because their interests
and passions will change and evolve swiftly. Take a
deep interest in whatever they love and be there to
be their champion on whatever it is.

» *Help them make Decisions in Advance in the special journal you give them.* Once it is explained
and established, stay interested and get an update
regularly.

The bottom line is that each grandchild is unique, and
whether you have one of them or a dozen, you want to think
of them not as a group, but as separate and distinctive—
equally valued, but not all treated the same—known and
appreciated for their individuality.

BEING Their Champion

ONE WHO GIVES CONFIDENCE, SELF-WORTH, AND
AN APPRECIATION FOR WHO THEY REALLY ARE—
AND WHO THEY CAN BECOME

"Championing"

O ne of the most fun and most natural steps in becoming a proactive GRANDfather is to be a *champion* for your grandkids.

This is not the kind of champion we see on the podium after winning an Olympic event or the player that gets carried off the field after winning the game. This is where the word "champion" becomes a verb as well as a noun, and where you become the person who elevates others as their advocate, encourager, supporter, defender, protector, and opportunity-maker. This is the kind of championing where you stand back, jury from the podium, invisible, and cheer for the person you have mentored and trained.

In this context, who would you rather champion than your grandchildren?

How do we become their champions? How do we become their biggest cheerleaders and strongest supporters and encouragers?

In keeping with the "being" theme of this book, a good place to start is by thinking about the question, "What kind of champion do you want to *be* to your grandkids?" Here are some suggestions to consider:

Babies to eight years old: Be their *ringmasters*

Eight to sixteen: Be their *buddies*

Sixteen and up: Be their *consultants*

CHAMPIONING BY AGE GROUP

BE A RINGMASTER FOR GRANDKIDS UNDER 8

In a good old circus, the ringmaster was out there having a good time and drawing us all into that good time. He appreciated every act and led the applause. He introduced us to the joy!

With young grandkids, just show them a good time. Take them places, show them things, spoil them a little (but always in concert and communication with their parents). Enjoy them, and let them enjoy you! Be their ringmasters in the circus of their young lives.

BE A BUDDY FOR THE ONES BETWEEN 8 AND 16

Kids have a lot of friends, but during these years, they need a special kind of buddy—one who knows them, one who loves them unconditionally, one who has always believed in them, one who is always there for them, one whom they can trust and confide in, and to whom they can tell anything and everything.

Also, with these "middle-aged" kids, moving into and through adolescence, you've got to be tech savvy and online. And email won't cut it! Just be, electronically, whatever and wherever they are. And as they evolve from Facebook and Twitter to Instagram or Pinterest or Snapchat or whatever comes next, try to evolve with them.

BE A CONSULTANT TO THOSE OVER 16

Often when kids get to this age, their parents still treat them as kids—and they need someone to treat them as adults. They need someone who wants to know their opinions and who respects those opinions.

With these upper teens, establish a relationship of trust in which they will ask for your advice, or at least listen to it. Explain to them that a consultant is not a manager or someone who tells you what to do or pushes you around. A consultant is someone with a lot of experience who can help you with your goals and help you get what you want and become what you want to be.

THE REMARKABLE POWER OF PRAISE AND COMPLIMENTS

There is a simple principle that I finally learned late in my dad-hood with my children, but oh I apply and practice it now as a granddad with my grandchildren! It is simply this: *Kids thrive, flourish, and blossom in the light of thoughtful, specific, sincere compliments, particularly from their grandfathers!*

The basic fact is that a certain amount of insecurity is part of childhood and part of growing up. Kids have the tendency to compare themselves a lot to their peers; and unfortunately, adults seem to always be comparing them to each other, judging them, evaluating them, and grading them. In media and social media, kids constantly see other kids who are better looking, more talented, more outgoing, and (surely they must be) happier than they are.

In this reality, sometimes a well-placed compliment, coming from a grandpa, can have a powerful and lasting positive influence.

Like I said, I first realized this as a dad, and it was connected to one particular experience. One of our sons, just six or seven years old, was really droopy and down one day. I lifted him up on my lap and asked him what was wrong. He said something about not being picked in a playground game when kids were "choosing up." Then, he teared up a little and said he wasn't any good at anything and that even his little brother was better at basketball and smarter in school than he was.

Desperate to help him feel better and show my love and approval, I did a spontaneous and kind of odd thing. There was a pen on the table by where we were sitting, and I picked it up and held his hand open, palm up, and wrote a "B" on the tip of his index finger.

"What's that, Dad?" he asked, his curiosity stopping his tears.

"Well, I was just sitting here thinking of all the things YOU are good at—things you are better at than your brother, in fact, better at than anyone in the family."

"Like what? What is the B?"

"You can always make the baby stop crying. You are so good with your baby sister. When no one else can make her happy, you can!"

It was true, he really did have that gift, and he started to brighten up, looking at the B on his finger. Then I wrote an "S" on his pointing finger and told him that he had the most wonderful, natural smile, and that many people had told me that they thought he had one of the brightest, handsomest smiles of any kid they had ever seen. He responded with a big one, and held his hand up higher. I put an "H" on the next finger and told him that when I came home from work, he gave the best, warmest hugs, and that they always made me feel so good. Then I put a "P" on his little finger and an "A" on his thumb, and we talked about how good he was at puzzles and what an amazing artist he was.

His face and his whole countenance brightened up so visibly that I stayed with it, giving details and examples and embellishment on each letter. "Seriously, son, when you draw things, you do so with much more detail than most kids— you get the fingers and thumbs just right on people you draw. And your clouds and sky look so realistic—you are an amazing artist."

We must have talked for a half hour about his talents and the things he was good at, and it could have gone on and on. He was focused. He sat there on my lap not moving a muscle, soaking in the compliments like a sponge, growing happier and more animated by the minute.

What a great opportunity we have to do this same kind of thing with a grandchild.

We can write letters on his fingers; we can take her for a little walk with the sole purpose of talking about some specific aptitude or quality we like; we can write him a handwritten compliment on something we have noticed.

Again, remember, kids get judged a lot in their world, by their peers, by their teachers, and by their parents—judged, graded, disciplined, corrected, criticized. They deserve one person in their lives that sees only the good, someone in whose eyes they can do no wrong, someone who sees all their good points and none of the bad, someone who is truly their champion . . . and no one is better positioned to be that person than their grandfather.

SPECIAL RITUALS FOR CERTAIN AGES

You can have a set of personal "rites of passage" with each of your grandkids—special rewards or things they get to do with you as they reach certain ages. Having a plan or a strategy for these will put you in close contact with a grandchild at important times and allow you to be very practical about championing him or her at various stages.

Let me use my own setup as an example, not necessarily wanting you to follow it exactly (although there is no restriction against that) but hoping that it might spur your own ideas about what you and your grandkids might enjoy or benefit from.

At age four, I tell them "Mirrorland" stories and give them their own Mirrorland name. Mirrorland is a magical place that they can see into whenever they look into a mirror. In my Mirrorland, there is a family remarkably similar to the Eyres, but they are called the Doolittles, and the guy who looks like me in there is Crunk Doolittle. In my stories, the main Doolittle character is the one who is very similar to the grandchild I'm telling the story to, and Crunk is always there, and they have some great times together.

At age six, I build a "treasure chest" with each one. We do this at our lakeside vacation place, and it involves cutting up plywood and using wood glue and nails and some hinges and a lock hasp and a nice combination lock that we get at the nearby hardware store. The grandchild helps every step of the way, and especially does a lot in the sandpaper stage and the painting stage. Kids treasure these treasure chests and keep everything from their baby teeth to their tooth fairy money in them. More importantly, they remember that we made them together.

At age seven, I give them a "Bear Lake Rock." Bear Lake is our summer vacation place, and I found some polished rocks with the same hue of blue. During the summer of the year when my grandkids turn seven, I take each of them on a hike and we talk a lot about their life and their current "happys" and "sads." I tell them how much I love them and how special they are to me. We discuss the things they are good at, and I take notes in a special notebook. Then, I present them with a Bear Lake Rock and tell them to keep it in a safe place—probably in their treasure chest that we made the year before, and to pick it up and rub its smooth surface once in a while so that it can always remind them of the things they are good at and of how proud their grandfather is of them.

At age eight, I tell him or her the first two "Grandfather's secrets." There is a whole chapter in this book (chapter 7) on Grandfather's secrets, but it is at age eight that they get to hear the first two, one of which has to do with happiness and the other with prayer. I tell my grandchildren that I think eight is a magic age when they can think and be treated like an adult, so it is the beginning of me sharing with them ten secrets, all of which will be revealed by the time they are sixteen.

At age ten, I take each of them to "Singletree" which is a lone cedar tree growing near the top of a hill above the lake that has no other trees on it. As we hike to Singletree, we talk about how kids their age sometimes need to stand alone against the crowd and do what they know is right, even when the others are doing something else. We talk about examples, from shoplifting to bullying to lying. When we get to the tree, I tell them Grandfather's secret number five, which is "SINGLE TREE: You are unique and there is only one of you. Find your place and grow into all you can be. Seek a life of broadening and contributing." We compare him or her to the tree and talk about courage.

At age eleven, I expand on that thought of "broaden and contributing." We define the two words. (*Broadening* meaning education, travel, and experience that will help them see and understand the world better, and *contributing*, meaning to help other people every chance we get.) I then tell them that I have $500 for them, which I will give them when they show me a written plan for how they propose to use $250 for broadening and $250 for contributing. It's amazing the kind of proposals I get back, from paying for a class on astronomy to sponsoring a child in Ethiopia through an aid organization.

As each grandchild turns twelve, I give them a special diary. They may have had other diaries, but this is a very nice, leather-covered one, and we turn to the back of the diary and mark the last page, "Decisions in Advance" (which was detailed in chapter 1). I explain that most decisions can be made early, and that we make much better choices when we think things through in advance, rather than waiting for the temptations and peer pressure that may come at the moment of the decision.

At age thirteen, each grandchild gets a motorhome trip with Linda and me. If two grandkids are turning thirteen within a year of each other, we take them together. It's usually just two or three days, often just after our family reunion, and we have so far experienced Yellowstone Park, Las Vegas, and a big amusement park in Utah for our first three motorhome trips. This idea actually came from a wonderful mentor of mine who told me that he had taken a private motorhome trip with each one of his twelve grandchildren and that it was the most important step in getting to know each of them, one on one.

At age fifteen, I love doing a "virtual college tour" with a grandchild. They are just into high school at this age, and it is possible for them to think beyond a little bit and begin to contemplate their university and college possibilities. We make a list of possible colleges they might want to go to, and we look up pictures of them and lists of what majors and fields of study they offer. We look at pictures of the dorms, the cafeterias, and the sports and music programs. We think of it as an introduction to college possibilities, and it lays the groundwork for me to be a kind of college consultant over the next two or three years as they prepare and decide. This is really the parents' job and the parents' prerogative, but if it isn't happening, and if the parents welcome your involvement, why not?

Summary and Guidelines

To review, here are some things to remember as you become your grandkids' champion:

» *Get to know the individual.* What are his or her gifts and interests? Who do you see this youngster becoming, and how can you help? Be careful that you don't become a "controlling champion," who tries to dictate a child's future, imposing your own vision on them as an extension of your ego. Ask questions and be willing to be surprised.

» *Champion your grandkids differently at different ages.* Be the ringmaster for the little ones, the buddy for the middle ones, and the consultant for the older ones.

» *Be in teamwork with the parents.* Make sure that the parent or parents know of and welcome your support. Have their backs. Don't be autonomous on this, but instead, ask them what they believe their child needs and where they need help. It's incredibly easy to overstep, so be sensitive to the parents' desires and boundaries. All of chapter 3 is about this sensitivity.

» *Set up some rituals or rites of passage.* Put together a schedule of what you want to do with grandkids as they reach certain ages and give your grandkids the joy of anticipating these things before they happen and remembering them long afterward.

» *Consider how you can be the most help and then make a plan.* Will it be spending time together, going out together twice a month? Will it be making sure that you're there for all the big events in the child's life? Will it be creating a matching fund for education? What will it be for you and for that particular grandchild?

» *Follow through.* You can make your greatest impact through consistency and longevity. Letting someone know you're there for them, whenever they need it for as long as they need it, is one of the most valuable contributions you can make to anyone of any age.

The fact is that we can and should play a powerful role in teaching our grandchildren to live for responsibility and reputation rather than ease and entitlement (more on this and on teaching timeless values to our grandchildren in the next chapter). Our family, and the legacy we leave, will not be measured by how rich we are or how many titles we had, but by the family we started and the caliber of those family members. One of the worst and saddest things we can do is abdicate our role as grandparents, becoming passive and uninvolved instead of proactive and highly aware and involved with this precious third generation.

This chapter has been a bit heavy with tasks and involvement, but remember: you are not trying to do everything all at once, and you can just pick ideas that appeal to you now and that fit the age and needs of your grandkids now. You can save the other ideas for later.

■ GRANDPARENTING □
CHAPTER 3

BEING A TEAM MEMBER AND A ROLE PLAYER

ONE WHO UNDERSTANDS THAT PARENTS ARE THE
COACHES AND KIDS ARE THE STARS, BUT WHO
CAN STEP IN TO PLAY SPECIFIC NEEDED ROLES
AND TO FILL IN WHEN THERE ARE VOIDS

Unless you are raising your grandchild (as many grandparents do these days—and in which case you probably need a parenting book), it is essential to see your role as a supplement and a supporter to *your* child, who is the parent. Any efforts you make that are counter to or critical of a parent's parenting are likely to be counterproductive.

What kind of an empty-nest dad are you?

It's important to begin with this question—because it is the quality of your relationship with your adult children that will determine how big a factor you can be in the lives of your grandchildren.

Most of the thirty-five million baby boomer dads in this country (about five million male boomers are not parents) have entered or are about to enter this new landscape of *empty-nest fathering*. And while it's natural for any parent to dread the day when a child leaves the home to be on his own (though moms are usually more troubled by this than dads), it's also natural to look forward to the freedom you'll have when your kids move on and you have less day-to-day responsibility for them.

If you're an average baby boomer, you will be a dad for sixty-plus years of your life, and only about twenty of those years will be spent parenting your kids while they live with you. You'll spend two-thirds of your fatherhood as an empty-nest dad, and much of that time you will also be a granddad.

And being a good granddad starts with being a good empty-nest dad.

Two Ways to Fail:
Abdicate or Arbitrate

There are two perfectly predictable ways to fail at empty-nest fatherhood, and, frighteningly, most of us are headed directly for one or the other. Ironically, they are the exact opposite of each other—yet each is a virtual guarantee of the deterioration of your relationship with your grown children.

One way is to *abdicate*—to simply quit parenting once your kids leave home, to have no strategy or plan about what you will or won't help with, to step totally aside, and give them complete independence unless or until they come to you with a problem, and then hope you'll find a way to help. This option, obviously, eliminates any meaningful role you would play as a grandfather.

The other way to fail is to *arbitrarily* lay down a pattern or set of standards—how much financial help they'll get, what responsibilities they'll take, and what ones you'll keep—all *without* the input or agreement of your kids.

I remember one dad we know on the first extreme who had a little send-off party each time one of his three children went off to college. It was like a celebration, a bon voyage—a good-bye party for the child and a retirement party for him. The tone was, "Okay! I'm done, good luck. Try not to bother me, but if you really need something, call and I'll see if I can help."

Another dad, a single father, was the complete opposite. With the help of his attorney, he drafted a document that laid out not only a trust account and a precise schedule of when his children would receive what funds, but also a schedule of when they would visit home, when and how they would communicate by phone, text, and email, how he expected them to budget their time and their money, and where he expected them to be in their professional careers by the end of the decade.

Most fathers don't pursue either of these extremes intentionally or directly, but most do gravitate gradually toward one or the other—to *abdicate* or to *arbitrate*. Once again, both of these courses are guaranteed to drive dads and children apart and to severely limit the amount of influence or help you can be to your grandkids! What is needed instead is a carefully planned and communicated middle course involving a well-discussed and agreed-upon *strategy* of how the relationship, the independence, and the assistance will evolve as your child goes through the phases of moving out, going to school, working, and starting his or her own family. It is like a spectrum where we need to pull ourselves to the middle rather than be sucked to one end or the other:

abdicate:	consult and communicate:	arbitrate:
Back off, disengage, and just wait for needs and problems	Develop an agreed-on strategy that balances growing independence with gradually decreasing assistance	Lay down rules according to what you want and enforce them arbitrarily

As you read this chapter, I hope you will be attracted to the middle possibility and that you will see the opportunity and the joy of communicating and working with your kids to develop a plan for your ongoing relationship with them. Part of that planning will be a teamwork effort on how to parent and grandparent the grandkids.

I also hope that you develop a real fear of the two extremes and realize that it is abdicating or arbitrating that *distances* family relationships and eventually cuts off parent from child, child from parent, and grandchildren from grandfather.

It is in the middle ground of communication and cooperative commitment where you will develop the ideas and strategies for being involved and influential with your grandkids.

THE FOURTH STAGE

What is the best way to think about and conceptualize grandfathering and empty-nest fathering? First of all, try to view it as a fourth and completing phase or stage of a father's stewardship. First-stage dadhood is babies and preschoolers—the incredibly formative time when children acquire 80 percent of their cognitive ability and need an incredible amount of parenting attention. Second-stage fathering is the elementary school years, which is sometimes the least turbulent and worrying phase, but also the most opportunistic time to teach children responsibility and values. Third-stage fathership is the adolescent and teen years when children transition into decision-making young adults.

And then comes fourth-stage fathering, the longest stage by far—beginning when children first leave home and continuing . . . and continuing . . . and continuing, right through the wonderful part that includes grandparenting and on into years when your children essentially become your peers.

Why acknowledge, prioritize, and work at empty-nest fathering and grandparenting? Some of the answers are obvious: Your children are still your children, your *stewardship*, the biggest part of your heart. And your grandchildren are your legacy. Some reasons are less obvious, but equally important because they have to do with the most fundamental goal of happiness that resides in and revolves around family. The most powerful reason for doing your level best at empty-nest fatherhood and grandfatherhood is that those efforts will have more to do with the long-term well-being of your kids, of your grandkids, of your family, and of yourself than anything else you can do.

STAYING CLOSE BY BACKING OFF

Remember that when your children marry, they're not just under a different roof; they're part of a whole new and different organization. They're not just playing a road game; they're on a new team. The Bible says it best; they must now *leave* you and *cleave* to their spouse, to their partner. This priority shift, this emotional leaving and cleaving, can be a traumatic transition for your child, even if he or she has lived away from home for some time. They have just jumped over an invisible barrier out of your immediate family and into their own.

You and your child are now parts of each other's extended families.

Often, it is particularly hard for dads to give their daughters away, and to approve fully and openly of the guy who will essentially take your place as the most important man in that daughter's life.

But that is the amazing thing about families—they expand forever without contracting. They break the law of equal action and opposite reaction, because they're always additive and never subtractive. Your child gets married and starts a new, additional family, yet he is still part of your family, and his wife is added to your family. Net result: a larger family for you and a new family besides, and soon, hopefully, grandkids. And so it goes, on and on. You really don't lose a daughter; you really do gain a son, not to mention the blessing and delight of grandchildren.

The things you have to work to equalize and to balance are your time and your priorities. Your family will keep growing, but your time and your mental energy won't grow along with it. You'll have the same finite number of hours and the same amount of effort (and maybe a little less energy as time goes by), and you'll have to spread them thinner and over a larger number of family members. And your now-married son or daughter will (and should) devote most of his or her family time to the new spouse and new family.

Once we dads see this process clearly and accept it, we can be happy in our evolving role. We can let go gladly of control and responsibility and yet still preserve closeness and confidence. With gratitude and grace, we can step nimbly aside and into the remarkably joyful roles of trusted adviser and friend.

And within that carefully constructed dynamic, you have positioned yourself to be an involved, supportive, proactive grandfather.

Of course, there are cases where separation or estrangement or enmity is deep, and some of the ideal scenarios we have been talking about may seem like pie in the sky; but time is on your side if you begin to make amends and to move toward better relationships.

The Communication That Fosters Teamwork

The best way I know to get going on this consulting role and to make it positive for your children, as well as for your grandchildren, is to invite your child and his or her spouse out for dinner at a very nice restaurant (your treat) and to have a very specific agenda that I like to call a "Five-Facet Review."

Pick a classy place to eat that is quiet and conducive to conversation, and in that environment, steer the discussion along the following path:

1. I love your kids (my grandkids) so much and want to be a positive influence in their lives, as well as a support and supplement to you as their parents. You are in charge, you have the stewardship, and I just want to explore ways that I can help that will fit in with your goals.

2. I know it all starts by really knowing the kids and understanding what they need and what you are concerned about, so I wanted to just sit here with you during dinner and take notes and have you teach me more about my grandkids. Then, I hope you will share with me what your worries are and how I might help.

3. If it's okay, can we talk about each of the kids, one at a time, and in a framework where I can organize my notes? I think of it as a "Five-Facet Review." Starting with James, can you just tell me what comes to your minds about how he is doing physically, mentally, socially, emotionally, and spiritually? Just stream of consciousness and maybe allow me to ask a couple of questions here and there so I really get up-to-date.

4. So, first, how is James doing physically?

Take notes, ask questions, and focus your thought on each facet of each grandchild. Draw the parents (your child and in-law child) out and try hard to grasp not only where each grandchild is, but how the parents feel and where their concerns lie.

When you finish the Five-Facet Review, express your appreciation and compliment the parents on how well they know their children. Ask about their goals with each child and about their biggest challenges and frustrations. Reiterate that you don't want to interfere—on the contrary, you want to support them and see if there are areas where you can help with their goals or help out in areas of concern.

In this setting and with this approach, your kids will open up and ask for your help on certain things, and even if they don't, they will feel your concern and appreciate the fact that you are not judging them or wanting to interfere—only to support and help. You will likely go away with some good ideas on things you can do with the grandkids, and you can share your desire to be their champion, to build them up, and to do your part to build their self-esteem and develop their talents.

Make it clear to your kids that you will always be there for them and for the grandkids; and assure them that there is nothing on which they should fear asking for your help.

Suggest that you might want to repeat the "Five-Facet Review" with them in a few months just to keep updated and keep yourself informed enough to really be a meaningful help with the grandkids.

How much you can do and how often you can do it will be partly determined by how far away you live from your kids. If they are far away, you may have to have much of your contact be electronic, but we live in a world of FaceTime and Skype, where being close is much more a factor of desire and determination than it is of distance. The Five-Facet Review works nearly as well on Skype as it does in person

TEACHING YOUR GRANDCHILDREN VALUES

One of the areas where you and your parent-kids may conclude that you can best help and influence your grandkids is in the arena of teaching them about basic values. These values may be lived and exemplified in their homes (or may not in some cases), but children need a separate, outside voice reinforcing, elaborating, and explaining the importance and the practice of certain basic values. It is a mistake to assume that kids will naturally and instinctively gravitate toward the honesty, loyalty, responsibility, respect, restraint, and other values you want them to have. Teaching basic values has to be a deliberate goal of parents and grandparents.

Many years ago, Linda and I coauthored a book called *Teaching Your Children Values*, which became a national *New York Times* #1 bestseller. The reason parents liked it, I believe, was its simplicity. It set forth twelve universal values and suggested that families focus on one of them each month. The formidable challenge of helping kids to internalize the values that protect them and govern their choices and their progress in life seemed manageable when it was approached one value at a time, one month at a time.

Today, we live in a world where strong, basic values are needed more than ever in children's lives. And it is a world where parents are busier and more distracted than ever before and where most of them would welcome a grandfather who would step in and be an influential and direct teacher of values.

The twelve values from that earlier book are as follows. (As you review them, ask whether their practice is one of the legacies you want to leave within your grandchildren and whether the internalizing of these values is perhaps the best protection and stabilizing influence, and the most reliable aid in decision-making that they could have.)

1. Honesty
2. Loyalty and Dependability
3. Respect
4. Love
5. Unselfishness and Sensitivity
6. Kindness and Friendliness
7. Courage
8. Peaceability
9. Self-reliance and Potential
10. Self-discipline and Moderation
11. Fidelity and Chastity
12. Justice and Mercy

What if you were to focus on just one of these values each month with your grandchildren?

What if you told them that you had twelve gifts you could give them, or twelve wishes you could make come true within them, or twelve things you believe would make their lives happier and their decisions better?

Pose the values (and describe them) as twelve ways to be happy, twelve ways to be trusted and liked by others, and twelve ways to feel good about yourself. Tell your grandkids that you plan to focus on one of them each month and tell them some stories and have some little chats about each one as its month comes up.

You can do this in person if a grandchild lives close enough, or by text, email, FaceTime, and Skype if he or she lives too far away to get together each month.

Now, if the idea is appealing, but if it seems a bit over-whelming or impractical, here is one thing to make it easier.

Back when we wrote the book and in the years following, we worked with a group of playwrights and artists who took each value and put it into an engaging story, full of music and drama and humor, and aimed at kids between eight and fourteen. They were produced as audio stories with the goal of engaging kids' imaginations so powerfully that they would listen to them over and over during their designated month.

The whole thing succeeded beyond our expectations. The stories are so compelling that kids don't think of them as lessons—just as entertainment. Yet the designated value for each month comes through strongly, and kids actually experience the feelings and consequences of each value vicariously as they are listening. We found that the age range of appeal was even broader than we had hoped. Five- and six-year-olds were listening to and loving them, and while they didn't get the full meaning, they got parts of it. And fifteen- and sixteen-year-olds were listening, too, though not usually admitting it.

These monthly values-stories are being used by parents around the world and today are also being used more and more by grandparents who take on the challenge of teaching their grandkids values.

One good way to go about it is to introduce the values and the idea of one-per-month in the summertime and plan to work on and talk about one value each month over the course of the coming school year. The schedule could be set up like this:

1. Honesty (Initial adventure: Listen to this one first in
   August before kids go back to school. It will set up
   the schedule for the coming school year)
2. Peaceability (September)
3. Self-reliance and Potential (October)
4. Self-discipline and Moderation (November)
5. Fidelity and Chastity (December)
6. Loyalty and Dependability (January)
7. Respect (February)
8. Love (March)
9. Unselfishness and Sensitivity (April)
10. Kindness and Friendliness (May)
11. Courage (June)
12. Justice and Mercy (Concluding adventure: Listen to
    this one in July and use the summer to reflect back
    on each of the values and to decide to repeat them
    month-by-month during the year ahead.)

The monthly stories are called "Alexander's Amazing
Adventures," and each one follows a boy named Alexander
and a girl named Elle as they face common, everyday situations, choices, and behavioral dilemmas—but then they
morph into a Prince and a Princess in a larger-than-life world
called Inland, where their values choices can essentially save
the planet. Kids, as they listen to the stories and the music,
come to realize that the little things they face each day are
actually the same things that Alexander and Elle face in
Inland, where they are the Prince and Princess. Each story
provides a lot to talk about and many things to discuss. You

should try to listen to each story with your grandchild early in the month and then to have it on his or her phone or iPod so it can be listened to (by both of you) several more times as the month goes by.

Listen to the first adventure (on honesty), and you will be hooked. More importantly, your grandchild will also become addicted. Stories are the best way to teach, and these are exceptional stories indeed.

Getting the stories is easy. Visit valuesparenting.com and become a member, and then download the stories at valuesparenting.com/alexander/. You can sample the stories there before you sign up and assure yourself that they will "work" with your grandchild.

Summary and Guidelines

In review, here are five things to remember and to focus on:

» *Work first at becoming a good empty-nest parent.*
Few men are good grandfathers without also being good empty-nest dads. If you really care about your grandkids, you need to work *through* your kids.

» *Don't abdicate or arbitrate.* Instead, find the middle ground of listening, communication, and teamwork.

» *Accept your new role.* Be highly proactive and involved with your kids and their families, but recognize that they are autonomous and in charge now, and that you are the backup and supplement.

» *Hold Five-Facet Reviews* with your kids to learn and understand more about your grandkids.

» *Take a special, active role in teaching grandchildren values.* Decide on what values you want to teach and set up an organized system for doing so.

Thinking this all through—these new roles and new opportunities and new paradigms—can make you a highly useful "senior consultant" in your family and can make all the other suggestions and approaches in the remaining chapters work.

BEING the Connecting Link

ONE WHO CONNECTS GRANDKIDS TO THEIR
ANCESTORS AND SHARES A FAMILY NARRATIVE
THAT CAN BUILD THEIR LARGER IDENTITY AND
ENSURE THEIR RESILIENCE

Oil Paintings, Trees, and Stories

Years ago, I painted the only oil painting of my life. It is a large tree with lots of branches and lots of roots. It is painted so that there is an above-ground part and an underground part. Above is the tree itself, with my and Linda's picture on the trunk and one of our children's pictures on each of the main branches. Below, on the underground part of the painting, are the symmetrical roots—four of them coming down from the trunk and each splitting into two to form a second root-level of eight, and then, each splitting again to create the lowest level of sixteen roots.

We put the best headshot photos we could find of our parents (our children's four grandparents) on the first four roots, and of our grandparents (our children's eight great-grandparents) on the next deeper root-row of eight. And through a bit of "Family Search" research, we were also able to find photos of each of our eight great-grandparents (our kids' sixteen great-great-grandparents.)

Then, we compiled the stories we had heard and the ones we were able to find on genealogical and ancestry websites, and we wrote up each of them as a children's story, in children's language. We tried to find and write at least one story about each of the twenty-eight people in the roots (below-ground) part of the painting. These twenty-eight noble souls are our kids' grandparents, great-grandparents, and great-great-grandparents. Having their individual pictures visible on their individual roots on our family tree is what introduced these wondrous people to our children; and finding one interesting story from each of their lives is what helped our kids to feel some familiarity, to feel like they really knew each of them a bit.

It was the stories that did it—simple stories that our kids could relate to, which we wrote up in kids' language. Here is one of those stories to illustrate the point.

GRANDPA DEAN AND THE CAR WRECK

Your Grandpa Dean, who was my dad, lived in a little town in Wyoming. He was so excited when he turned sixteen and got his driver's license. The first time his dad (your great-grandpa Howard) let him take the car, he went on a date to a movie with a girl he liked. After he took her home, he was driving back to his house and going a little too fast, because it was almost midnight and that was his curfew. He drove over a hill on the slippery street and the car skidded into another car that was parked in front of the town's one little hotel. It dented the other car a bit, but there was no one around and all the lights were out in the hotel. Dean couldn't see any damage on his dad's car, so he just left and drove home.

By the time he got home, though, he just didn't feel right and he knew he had to tell his dad. He woke up his dad and told him what happened. Great-grandpa Howard listened to Dean's story and told him that he was proud of him for following his conscience and wanting to do the right thing.

They got up early the next morning and drove back to the hotel before anyone was awake. They found the owner of the damaged car, and Howard paid to have it fixed. Dean saved the money from his paper route for nearly a year and paid his dad back. Even though it was hard, Dean felt good inside because he had done the right thing, told the truth, and followed his conscience.

Some of our children's other favorites were simple stories like "Grandpa Dan and the Cat That Came Back," about a cat that young Dan in Sweden kept trying to give away, only to have it find its way home; and "The Reason We're Not Billionaires," about great-great-grandpa Bingham, who was a sheep farmer who was bothered by all the red rocks on his homestead, never realizing that they were copper ore. The property is now the site of the largest open pit copper mine in the world.

Time passes, and now our children are parents of our grandchildren, and some have their own family trees in their own houses, and we are no longer the trunks. On these latest family trees, I am underground now on a root rather than above-ground on the trunk. And you know what? I like being a root. I think it puts me in a good position to tell my grandkids stories about their other roots.

Ancestors and Resilience

Research is now suggesting that one of the very best things we can do for our grandkids is to teach them about their ancestors and give them the identity-strengthening blessing of a real "Family Narrative."

We had lunch one day with *New York Times* writer Bruce Feiler, who told us in person what his research shows— namely that kids who feel a family identity larger than themselves and who know something about the lives of their ancestors are more confident and more resilient than those who don't.

Feiler likes to refer to an Emory University study, which concluded, "the more children know about their family's history, the stronger their sense of control over their lives, the higher their self-esteem."[2] He says that the most useful and beneficial types of family ancestor stories are "osculating"; that is, they tell about the hard times as well as the good times.

"Children who have the most self-confidence," the study concluded, "have a strong 'intergenerational self.' They know they belong to something bigger than themselves."

Some of the research on resilience actually included a study of children who had endured and survived a crisis like 9/11. Amazingly, of all the factors considered and measured, the one that was the most predictive of a child's resilience was how much he knew about his grandparents and great-grandparents.

You, as a grandfather, are perfectly positioned to create the kinds of family narratives that can make your grandkids stronger and more resilient.

2. Feiler, Bruce. "The Stories that Bind Us." *New York Times.* http://www. nytimes.com/2013/03/17/fashion/the-family-stories-that-bind-us-this-life.html

Start with a simple personal history. You can do it right out of your own memory. And you've probably got some pictures and stories of your own parents, grandparents, and great-grandparents that you can throw in.

Here is a little more detail on how it came together for me:

It started when I came across a couple of old journals, one that belonged to my father and one from my grandfather who emigrated from Sweden. The accounts (particularly the Swedish one) told of incredible hardships, but also of the adventure and triumph of sea voyages and pioneer treks. We told some of the stories to our small children and were amazed at how interested they were.

It prompted me to do a real "ancestor search." During that search, which was mostly online, but involved a few old albums and diaries from the attic, I came across little stories or incidents from their everyday lives. I wrote them in children's language and put them in a binder labeled "ancestor stories." Linda did the same with some of her grandparents who had emigrated from Switzerland and Denmark. For many years, those little accounts were our kids' favorite bedtime stories. And they gave us a chance to say things like, "That was your great-grandmother! She had a pretty hard life, didn't she—but an exciting one. She was a smart, strong woman. And you have her blood in your veins!"

We began this whole family narrative business with our kids when they were small. But it became even more effective with our grandkids! Linda does a little half-day "Grammie Camp" with them each summer when we get together for our family reunion. She tells them ancestor stories and lets them illustrate or write about the things they like about their ancestors in their own little journals. Kids love the notion that they came from somewhere; they like to begin to understand the rudiments of genetics and the fact that they inherit appearance, traits, and tendencies from those who went before them.

This really became vivid to me one evening at a family reunion a few years ago. We had been telling "ancestor stories" to the grandkids and some of them seemed particularly impressed and moved by a story about a great-grandmother who had endured a terribly hard emigration journey from Denmark and then, a trek with handcarts and covered wagons across the plains and through hostile Indian country to where they settled in the American West. Her husband and some of her children died on the journey, but she made it and became a wonderful elementary school teacher who educated and helped hundreds of children.

Later that same evening, I happened to be walking past the room where we had been telling the story and where the ancestor tree hung on the wall. The room was empty except for little eight-year-old Hazel who was standing in front of the tree, her finger tracing from her own picture on a high limb of the tree down through her parents limb and down through our trunk, and down into the roots of her grandparents. Hazel didn't notice me peeking in and, thinking she was alone, spoke loudly to herself as her finger reached the picture of her great-grandmother. "I'm one-eighth from YOU!" she declared. I heard pride in her voice—and a certain kind of strength and resilience.

One good place to tell kids the stories of their grandparents is in the places where the stories happened. It is fun in a very deep sort of way to arrange short day trips with one or two grandkids to a town where one of their ancestors lived and to actually walk where they walked and try to imagine what it was like back in their day.

Another good place (and often more convenient) is the cemetery where ancestors are buried. A quiet day in a beautiful cemetery can be a marvelous place to let a grandchild locate an ancestor's headstone, read the dates of his birth and death, and hear some of their stories. You can almost see the satisfaction and identity in their eyes as they begin to "get" who they are and where they came from.

IDENTITY

Another way to look at this whole family narrative business is through the lens of "identity" and the inherent need that kids have to be part of something bigger than themselves.

One reason adolescents join gangs is that they need this larger identity. The reason they want to follow a certain style or behave in a particular way is that they have an inherent need to be part of something larger than themselves—to fit into some bigger whole, to have something to rely on, to fall back on, and to belong to.

That "thing," of course, should be family. Not just their nuclear or household family, but their extended family—their ancestors—the progenitors whose genetics and traits and propensities they share. Knowing their roots makes them more secure and more resilient.

And that shouldn't surprise us. It is natural for a child who knows that her great-grandmother survived tough times to have a little more confidence in enduring some small crisis of her own. And a child who knows the stories of the successes of his great-great-grandparents takes on a little extra confidence in himself.

After we began finding and rewriting stories from our kids' grandparents and great-grandparents, we compiled them in an "Ancestor Book."

For us, the Ancestor Book was a big, old leather-bound book of blank paper that we got while we were living in England. In it, we write down the stories we know about various forebearers, in children's-story language. We adopted the stories from journals and diaries and from the oral traditions we had heard as kids. We kept adding stories and gave each story an exciting title like "Grandma Ruth and the Grisly Bear" and "How This Mountain-Moving Family Stayed Together on the Pioneer Trail." Our young children illustrated the stories with little drawings of stick figures and imagination.

And as I mentioned, these little bits of family history became our kids' favorite bedtime stories.

There has never been an easier time to create this kind of a family narrative. Websites like Ancestry.com make it convenient to locate the data on ancestors, and with a little cyber-digging and contacting older relatives who are still alive, it is surprisingly easy to find stories about most of these noble folks to whom we owe so much.

An even better source, in my opinion, is familysearch.org, where you can enter whatever small amount of information and dates you have about an ancestor and be linked to the most extensive genealogical research source on earth to connect with additional data. This site will put your family tree into "fan" form and allow you to click through to all available information about preceding generations and also access any available photos, documents, and stories about that person. (Beware, this site is addictive!)

Summary and Guidelines

It is hard work, but by doing the family research and creating the stories and the family tree, you can make a huge difference in how your grandchildren view themselves. Here are the three things to focus on:

1. *Understand the power and influence of Family Narrative.* In this transient, disposable, fast-changing world of ours, kids desperately need to be connected, and the best thing to connect them to is their extended family and ancestors.

2. *Do the research and make the tree and write the storybook.* Start with a simple chart that shows your grandparents and great-grandparents and any data you can find on them. Then, put it onto some kind of big chart or "tree" with pictures. Write the stories into children's language for your grandkids.

3. *Have the conscious goal of giving your grandchildren the valuable gifts of identity and resilience.* Linking

the "branches" of your grandchildren to the roots of your forebears is one of the most enjoyable and most beneficial things you can do—for yourself as well as for them.

Just as your grandchildren will be the key and the substance of your future legacy, you can, in turn, provide the key and the substance of their link to the past and their larger-than-self-identity. Think of yourself as the storytelling connector of branches to roots.

BEING Their Consultant

One who listens and lifts and helps them set and reach their own goals

Learning to be a Consultant Rather than a Manager

This chapter is particularly for grandfathers with teen-aged grandchildren. Start by focusing on two words that describe and define two very different roles:

Manager: A person in charge; with responsibility, with authority; one who decides and directs.

Consultant: A person who helps other people with their goals; one who advises and assists.

What a difference! With small children, parents and grandparents are the managers. That's what you were to your kids early on, and that's what your kids are to your grandkids now. When we have young, growing children depending on us and in our care, the day-to-day responsibility is ours.

With grown children, and with grandchildren who are in their teens, it all changes—not only in degree, but in *kind*. A whole different type of relationship needs to evolve—one where we try to *respond* to their initiative, to help them with *their* goals, to back off and give them space to make their own decisions, but to be always willing and ready to help.

This is not an easy shift! Our dad-instincts are still to protect and to shelter . . . to manage. This inclination can undermine our grown children's independence, their motivation, and their confidence. And with grandchildren, our instincts are to give them everything and to simply "tell them what they need to know." But as grandkids reach their teens, what they really need you to be is a reliable consultant.

Consultant-style input complements and enhances their growing independence and leaves them with the positive incentives that come to anyone who feels entrusted with his or her own choices and decisions and directions.

Hopefully, with your grown children, you have moved away from the managerial role and into the consulting role. And now, or soon, you will have the opportunity to make that same transition with your grandchildren. You can actually even do it a little earlier (at a grandchild's younger age) than you did with your kids. With your children, you had to be the manager, at least in many respects, until they were mostly out on their own. But your grandkids have their own managers in their parents, which frees you up to take on the consulting persona earlier—during their teen years.

The most effective route away from managing and toward consulting is to ask questions. That is the prime skill of all good consultants. Ask (with positive interest and with no judgment) every question you can think of. Get inside your grandkids' heads and their hearts and understand where they're coming from. And learn to wait for the magic moments when *they* ask *you* for advice!

Asking Them to Ask

When advice is initiated by the giver, it can sound a lot like lecturing or judgment. But when it is asked for by the receiver, the whole feeling and chemistry changes. When we are asked for advice, for suggestion, for input, for guidance, it opens wonderful opportunities for involvement and for influence.

Imagine, for example, that you are concerned about how a grandson talks disrespectfully to his mother. If you confront the boy, even kindly and nicely, and suggest that he change his tone and show more respect for his mom, he is likely to feel defensive, and he is sure to feel that you have judged him and are critical of him. On the other hand, if he says he is concerned about his relationship with his mother (your daughter or daughter-in-law) and asks what you think he could do about it, you become his requested consultant rather than his unwelcome, critical "corrector."

The warm and trusting communication that opens up when advice is asked for is a huge asset to a relationship and can last a lifetime. Perhaps this is why the most frequent admonition in the Holy Bible is to "ask." And the admonition is almost always followed by the promise, "and ye shall receive." Apparently, even God knows that greater good can be done and more faith built when someone asks than when advice and direction is given unbidden. I like the notion that God's commandments are "loving council from a wise Father," and that even the ten Biblical commandments did not come until Moses asked for God's help and direction.

So how do we get our grandkids to ask?

Part of the challenge is that children these days just aren't very good at asking questions. Schools reward them for "right" answers, not for good questions. And kids often feel that any question they do happen to have can be easily answered by Google.

I've gone to some lengths to try to reverse these notions in my grandkids, and I try to start early. You might call it bribery, but sometimes when I'm around a young grand-child, under age eight, I have offered a dollar for every good, thoughtful question he can ask me. I've explained to them that in today's world, answers are cheap and easy, but really good questions are rare and incredibly valuable. Most tech businesses spring up from one really good question, and people who get good at asking questions become more observant and gather the information that keeps them free from a lot of mistakes.

As they get older, I've tried to tie these types of conversations with grandkids into an introduction of the word "consultant" and why I want to play that role with them. I explain that there is a big difference between a manager and a consultant in business. The manager is in charge, and he tells people what to do, which is usually good for them but not always pleasant. He sets goals and standards for them and expects them to reach and live up to what he has set. A consultant, on the other hand, is there to help people frame and accomplish their goals. The consultant listens first, instead of talking, and then makes suggestions rather than demands. I explain that their parents have to be their managers, particularly when they are small, and that we should all be grateful to parent-managers for taking care of us and keeping us safe.

Then, I suggest that what I can be, as a granddad, is their consultant. I explain that I've had a lot of experience and, believe it or not, I remember when their parents were their age and even when I was their age. Thus, I can listen to what they are doing or feeling or needing or trying to decide, and I can give them advice rather than commands, and they know that, whether they follow my advice or not, I will always love and accept them totally.

Once you introduce this concept of being a consultant to your teenaged grandchild, tie it in with the special notebook for each grandchild mentioned back in chapter 1. Let your grandchild see that you are so intensely interested in him that you make notes in your book whenever you talk to each other. Explain that you want to know and remember as much about him as you possibly can so that you will be able to give good advice when he asks.

In this conversation, stress that consultants usually cost a lot, but that your grandkid is lucky because he gets you for free.

Another very direct way to get grandkids to ask you questions is to frame a discussion or a "Grandpa date conversation" along the lines of taking turns with questions. First, you ask your granddaughter some questions about her life, taking notes and listening actively. Then, say that it is her turn and that she can ask you whatever she wants and you will try to answer honestly. With some kids, this opens up a flood of curiosity; with other, shyer ones, not much may come out the first time or two, but as you praise their questions and give them other opportunities, the beautiful aspect of "questions for each other" will make your relationship closer and closer as time passes.

THE NON-OFFENSE PACT

I'll be honest and tell you that my biggest problem with my own kids was giving too much advice. I'm a consultant by occupation and an advice-giver by nature, and I slipped into the trap of going from "manager" with my little children to "managing consultant" with my teenagers and continuing that pattern when they moved out and started their own lives.

And they resented it.

More than once, I had the older ones say to me, in essence, "Back off, Dad. We appreciate your advice, but you offer it too freely and too strongly."

I tried to pull back, to wait until they asked, and to just bite my tongue when I saw something I thought I could help on. But it was killing me. I felt that I couldn't let them walk into something I thought was harmful or let them "rediscover the wheel" on something that I already knew. So, I kind of went right on blasting them with advice whenever something occurred to me.

It was becoming a problem and undermining my relationship with them—until one summer we came up with a "pact." It was simple: They agreed to let me give advice on whatever I felt I had to and to "hear me out" and try not to be offended by the advice (or the implication that they needed it). In return, I agreed not to be offended if they did not follow the advice.

It was a simple pact, but it took the pressure off and showed mutual respect. Suddenly, I felt less compelled to give advice, and they felt less resistant to it when I gave it. What happened is that they started asking more and I started volunteering less. The whole chemistry got better. I now have this same pact with my teenaged grandkids.

It's actually much easier to give advice to our grandkids than to our kids. The grandchildren are generally not trying to prove anything, and they don't feel belittled or distrusted like our kids often did when we suggested things to them. But making "the pact" with grandkids is still a good idea, and one that shows them confidence and respect.

Take Little Trips or "Listening Dates."

Sometimes, all that is required to build a good consulting relationship with a teenaged grandchild is a little uninterrupted time.

The two best ways I know to get this kind of focus-time are short one-on-one road trips and little lunch or dinner dates.

Sometimes, something as simple as picking up a grandkid from school for his lunch hour and going to his favorite burger place for a half hour can yield some great interaction. Once you have set up and defined together the "consulting relationship" you want to have and perhaps decided on your "pact," you are in a position to start asking questions about what interests him most, about friends, about likes and dislikes in school, about goals for the school year, about summer plans, about favorite subjects, activities, movies, music, and on and on. Taking notes makes the conversations feel more serious and consequential and allows you, on a future occasion, to start with something like, "You know, since our lunch, I've been thinking about some things you said. . . ."

For a more in-depth "consulting session," take a little road trip together. Car time can be one of the best "opening up" environments. Kids seem to feel less pressure and often bring up things without being asked. And, as with all good consultants, you can use a little comment to find a passageway to deeper things. As mentioned earlier, just learn to use the word "Really?" and let him go on.

Don't give in to the natural instinct to give advice or input or lecture a bit every time you think of something. Just keep him talking and keep your use of "Really?" coming, and keep thoughts or your notes in your own head until the time feels right to suggest something.

Tell Them Stories about Their Parent

One surefire way to hold a grandkid's interest is to tell them stories about their parents when they were their age. It's hard for teens to actually imagine their parents as teens who actually felt and experienced some of the things they are feeling and doing now—but it is very beneficial and reassuring when they do.

Exercise your own memory and try to recall things about your daughter at fourteen while you are talking to your fourteen-year-old granddaughter. Use your memory to help your granddaughter feel closer to her mom and to open up more to you.

I was with my adolescent granddaughter not long ago, and I knew that her mom was feeling a lot of power-struggle going on with this strong-willed girl; I happened to mention to this granddaughter that her mom was pretty opinionated and difficult at her same age. I instantly had her attention, so I told her about a couple of disagreements I had had with her mom those many years ago, and how good she was at making her arguments and trying to get her way. As I related some little incidents, I could see the wheels turning and she started asking me other questions, like who her mom's first boyfriend was and what she used to like to do on dates.

I was careful to keep everything positive but to also make it real, and the whole discussion brought us closer together. (And I found out later that it also made the granddaughter feel more connected to her mom and helped the communication between them.)

Summary and Guidelines

As your grandchild becomes a teen, make a conscious effort to turn your bond into a consulting relationship. Here are five things to remember:

» *Understand the differences between a manager and a consultant*, and make a deliberate effort to move from one to the other as grandkids enter their teen years.

» *Tell grandkids how much you appreciate it when they ask questions*. Explain what consulting is and how much you are honored to be their consultant. Promise them that you will always be there for them and that they can ask you about anything without fear of judgment.

» *Enter into an "advice pact" with teen grandkids* so that they know you are only giving advice, not dictates or instructions and so that they know you will not be offended when they don't exactly follow all of the advice you give them.

» *Schedule lunches and "dates"* to have enough uninterrupted time together to allow the consulting relationship to develop and flourish.

» *Tell them stories about their own parents* to illustrate how "normal" they are and to reassure them that they are going through much of what their folks did and that they can share concerns with their parents, knowing that they have had similar concerns.

Remember that this consulting relationship you try to establish with your grandkids is not just another little phase. It is the kind of communication and trust you want to have with them for the rest of your life.

■ GRANDPARENTING □

CHAPTER 6

BEING an INDEPENDENCE-GIVER

ONE WHO WORKS OUT WAYS FOR THEM TO
EARN THINGS FOR THEMSELVES AND WHO
SUBSTITUTES GRIT FOR ENTITLEMENT

The Extreme Danger of Entitlement Attitudes

Don't we all worry, at least sometimes, about how our kids are raising our grandkids? And if the worry was to center on one thing, wouldn't it be the entitlement attitudes we often see in kids the same age as our grandchildren?

But how do you tactfully bring it up to your parent-children? How do you make any parenting suggestions without the risk of offending or getting shut off? And how do you do your own grandpa thing to help those grandkids learn about the importance of work, saving, delayed gratification, and self-reliance?

These were some of the questions in our minds as Linda and I wrote our recent bestselling book, *The Entitlement Trap: How to Rescue Your Child with a New Family System of Choosing, Earning, and Ownership.*

We were writing it for parents, of course, but make no mistake: we were also writing it for grandparents!

Here is the message of that book in a nutshell:

1. Kids are more entitled today than ever before. They think they deserve to have everything they want, right now, without waiting, and without working.

2. They think they have to have everything their friends have, including the latest gadgets and electronics.

3. With this kind of entitlement attitude, they begin to lose their motivation to work and to save and to

do their best. Their incentive and their gratitude are diminished, as well as their ingenuity and creativity.

4. We call it an "Entitlement Trap" because once kids develop this kind of attitude, it holds them back, and it is very hard to pull out of.

5. Media, consumer debt, and even government welfare can contribute to this entitlement trap, but the simple fact is that parents are most to blame. We are talking about well-meaning parents who want their kids to have everything their kids' friends have and who sometimes give too much "stuff" to make up for how little time they have to spend with them because they are working more and seeing their kids less.

6. The entitlement attitudes of today's kids go beyond what they think they deserve to *have*; it also gets into an attitude of thinking that they should be able to *do* whatever they want, which leads to all kinds of behavioral problems.

7. Along with the indulgence of parents, a key cause of entitlement in kids is that they do not perceive real ownership of anything, and without the pride of earned-ownership, there is no incentive to take care of things. Kids don't perceive ownership of their clothes or their toys. Why should they? They didn't work for them, didn't sacrifice anything for them, and probably didn't even choose them or pick them out. So, they throw them on the floor, lose them, and undervalue them.

8. Perceived ownership is the prerequisite to responsibility and the antidote to entitlement. And it's not only their toys and clothes that today's kids feel no real ownership of; it's also their values, their goals, and their choices.

9. The key to overcoming entitlement is to find ways to help kids feel real, earned ownership. This can be done by setting up a "family economy" with a payday instead of an allowance day. Kids have certain jobs they are responsible to do and to keep track of. How much they get when the family bank (some kind of big, impressive box or chest with a big lock on it) is opened up on Saturday is directly proportional to how much they have done!

10. The kids (starting as early as age eight) get a checkbook with checks they can write to take money out of the family bank and deposit slips to use to put money into the bank on payday. With their "earned money," they become responsible for buying their own stuff rather than begging for it. Having their own earned money translates into real ownership of what they buy with it, and they begin to take better care of their things. This pride of ownership changes their behavior as well as their attitudes.

11. This sense of ownership is then transferred to even more important things like decisions, grades, and even conflicts. What they own is what they feel responsible for and that is the beginning of true self-reliance.

What Can Grandfathers Do about Entitlement?

So, here we are as grandparents who love our grandkids, and we see their enormous potential. But we also see the entitlement attitudes that surround them and that swirl into their lives from the media, from their peers, and, too often, from their parents.

We want to be the factor that transforms, in our grandkids, the prevailing sense of entitlement into a stronger sense of responsibility!

So how can grandfathers be this factor? How can we make the difference?

First of all, consider giving your children-with-children a copy of *The Entitlement Trap* and encourage them to set up an "earning family economy" as the book suggests. Sweeten the encouragement by offering to match any money they put into their family bank when they set up a chore-based, savings-incentive, buy-their-own-stuff family economy like the book outlines. In this way, you will become a partner in a system that fights entitlement attitudes and begins the process of independence-gaining for your grandkids.

Secondly, whether or not you can get an earning-based family economy going in your kids' homes, be sure that your own financial interactions with your grandkids promote work and responsibility and earning rather than further entitlement.

Realize That You Give Them More by Giving Them Less

I know, I know! It is the prerogative of all grandfathers to spoil their grandkids a bit. And I agree with that little indulgence, particularly for little preschool grandkids. But once they get to be six, seven, or older, remember that everything you give them can advance a counterproductive entitlement attitude that you don't ever want to be a part of.

So here is one simple thing to STOP doing, and another thing to START doing:

» **Stop** giving them so much.
» **Start** making it possible for them to earn some things for themselves.

Set Up a Grandfather's Bank

If your children are not ready or able to set up a family bank and family economy, but you are in a position to do so, set up one of your own with their agreement and permission. Have a "Grandfather's Bank" for your grandkids from eight to fifteen years old who live reasonably close to you.

Once you have cleared the idea with the parents and listened to their inputs, follow this basic process:

1. Get a wooden chest or box of some kind—the more substantial and impressive the better. An inexpensive, secondhand store is a good place to look, or you could build it yourself. Get a big lock on it and maybe even label or name it as "Grandfather's

Bank" or "Jones Grandkids Savings Bank" or whatever you like.

2. Introduce the bank to any grandkids who are eight
   or older. Tell them that it is a place where they can
   save money and learn about earning and budgeting
   money wisely. Explain that the bank pays interest
   and explain interest as rent that the bank pays on
   your money that you keep there. Consider paying one percent per month interest. The monthly
   calculation will be a way to have a regular conversation each month with each grandchild who has an
   account in the bank.

3. Get a checkbook for each account holder. You probably have some old checkbooks around that you can
   use or you can get some extra ones from your bank.
   Put the kids' names on the checks, and show them
   how to get money out of the bank by writing a check
   or put it in by filling out a deposit slip.

4. Tell grandkids that they are welcome to put any
   money they want to earn interest on into the bank
   at any time, but that they can only withdraw it at the
   end of a month after interest has been added.

5. Explain that there will also be a special way that they
   can earn extra money to put in the bank. At the start
   of each school term, you will help them to set some
   goals in the three categories of grades, extracurric-
   ular, and character; and that while the best reward
   for their completion will be the satisfaction they get
   from meeting those goals, the bank will also pay

them a bonus for each goal they complete. Work out with each individual grandchild what the goals will be and what the bonus will be for meeting each one.

6. Tell the grandkids that the bank also offers short consulting sessions on saving and budgeting, which will show them how to plan what they do with the money they earn. As their financial consultant, recommend that they always save 20 percent of any gifts or anything they earn, and at the same time, as they take out the money to be saved, they also take out 10 percent to donate to a church or charity or other cause that they choose.

7. Consider setting up a separate "college savings account" in the Grandfather's Bank for each grandchild. In this special account, the money they put in is earmarked for college and can't be taken out until then—but it pays a much higher interest rate of, say, 10 percent per quarter.

Once again, it's important to coordinate these grandfather efforts with your kids, the parents, and to explain to them what your objectives are and be sure that they fit in with their own efforts to teach independence and overcome entitlement attitudes in the kids.

MATCHING GRANTS

With or without the Grandfather's Bank, consider establishing a Grandfather's Matching Fund, as you are able, to which grandkids can apply when they are trying to save up for higher ticket items like camps or other opportunities.

Sit down with the grandchild and talk about how great it is to earn and save to buy or pay for something, but that sometimes really good things just cost more than what a kid can save up. Explain that you, as their consultant and advisor, would like to help in those situations—not by giving money, but by supplying a match for the money the child has been able to come up with on his or her own.

Explain further that you now have a fund that can provide matching funds ("You have one hundred dollars, and the fund matches it with one hundred dollars.") for "worthy" purchases or experiences.

If the grandchild wants to go to a swimming camp, for example, and the cost is $180, if he or she has or can save $90 and writes a "matching grant proposal" on why it is a worthy expense and what the benefits of it would be, then the fund will match it with another $90 so that he or she will be able to go. Matching grants can also be applied to buy a smartphone or for any other purchases that the child can successfully explain as worthwhile and worthy of the matching grant.

We will discuss some further opportunities for grandfathers to help financially in other ways, particularly with older grandchildren, in chapter 9. The Grandfather's Bank and matching grants are among the first lessons for your grandkids, precursors to the financial management that they'll need to learn as they get older.

Summary and Guidelines

You may not win the big prize in the drama of changing your grandkids' entitlement attitudes, but you should be in the running for best supporting actor. Here is a brief review:

> » *Understand the dangers of entitlement* and the motivation and work ethic it can rob your grandchildren of, and realize that you can be the antidote.
> » *Develop a strategy to overcome entitlement and promote independence* by discussing the issue as an extended family and sharing ideas and working together to create a family economy that will teach earning, saving, and delayed gratification.
> » *Set up a Grandfather's Bank* that helps grandchildren learn about meeting goals, saving, and compound interest.
> » *Set up a matching grant* to give extra incentive to grandkids and to become the precursor of the additional financial facilitation discussed later in chapter 9.

This is essentially an opportunity to reverse what has come to be thought of as the usual role of grandfathers—namely to spoil, entitle, and unreasonably enable their grandkids. Instead of giving them too much freely, we can teach them to earn and do for themselves—and what could be a greater contribution than that?

BEING a
SECRET SHARER

ONE WHO TEACHES THE PRINCIPLES THAT
REALLY MATTER IN AN EXCLUSIVE,
EXCITING, AND SECRETIVE WAY

"Grandfather's Secrets"

All of us grandfathers are teachers in our hearts, and there are things we want to share with our grandchildren. But, how do we do it in a way that interests them and grabs their imagination?

When I asked myself this question, I knew that the key to success was to come up with something relevant and identifiable and to connect it to some kind of mystery and some kind of reward.

I knew the things I wanted to teach them—the legacies of insight that I wanted to leave them, but I didn't know how to get them interested or keep them interested.

As I often do, I resorted initially to a bit of bribery. I couched it by telling our three oldest grandkids, who were eleven, ten, and eight at the time, that there were four secrets I had learned that I wished I had known when I was their age. The word "secret" got to them a little, but I needed more—more intrigue and more motivation.

So, I found some rare South American stones at a rock hound place—polished rocks that I know were different than anything they had seen—and I named them the "Bear Lake Rocks." I told them that if they could memorize the four secrets I was about to tell them—and if they could give at least one example of how the secrets might play out in a real-life situation—that I would give each of them one of the Bear Lake rocks so that rubbing their soft, polished surfaces during the school year ahead would remind them of the secrets they had memorized.

I was getting there—there was a degree of intrigue in their faces, but I needed more. So I told them that, in addition to the special secret rocks, any of them who memorized the secrets and gave me an example of how the secrets could be applied would get a one hundred dollar bonus, and that if they remembered them until Christmas and could add an actual experience in applying each one by then, they would get another hundred dollars in their Christmas stocking.

Now I had them—especially since I had picked up three one hundred dollar bills as a visual aid.

The four initial secrets were:

1. "Most kids are waiting for someone to lead them, but they just don't know it yet."
2. "Good popularity comes from being nice to everyone, and it lasts. Bad popularity comes from only being nice to certain people, and it doesn't."
3. "Joy is the purpose of life and a choice you make."
4. "Blood is thicker than water, and cousins are more important than friends. We will always stay close to each other and set a good example for each other and be there for each other."

The first discussion we had together about these first four secrets was priceless. In the open, unguarded words of preadolescents, they talked about followers and leaders and about how hard it was to go against the crowd. They thought of examples among their friends of click-ish, "bad popularity." They had thoughts about how you could decide to be happy, even when you were having a bad day. They talked about how much they liked each other and how glad they were that their parents were siblings and that they would always be cousins.

When the reunion was over, they proudly took their rocks, and their money, and they promised to stay in touch from their respective homes in Boston, Utah, and Arizona. By Christmas, they each had some real-life examples to share on each of the secrets.

Time has passed, and there are now ten secrets—and I'm delighted to say that they are, to a degree at least, becoming self-fulfilling prophecies and are being passed on to younger cousins, with the older ones acting as tutors. We added one or two new secrets each summer at our reunion, each time having the same kind of "what does this mean and how could you apply it" discussion.

It wasn't a panacea, but it has helped on numerous levels, including in my relationship and relevance to each of them.

An Illustration

Let me share with you an email used to introduce the final secret to my older grandkids—who were in their upper teens—sent to them in the spring so that they could think about it a little before we gathered at the summer reunion. This one involves faith and a belief in God, and while you may choose a different format, a different formula, and different principles that you want to teach your grandkids, you can use this as one example of a direction you might go. The letter is a little long, but it may give you a better idea of what a grandfather's secret can be and how this can be a positive process of influencing grandchildren.

DEAR BLANK, BLANK, AND BLANK, (THREE ELDEST GRANDKIDS)

Oh, the memories we share,
You oldest three,
Here, there, and everywhere,
But especially at Bear Lake
The sunsets,
The Treasure Chests
(working away on them together at the pavilion),
Good Dog Able (only you oldest grandkids
have this memory),
The lake and the sand,
The skiing and the sailing,
The storms that turn the lake to slate
and the sky to charcoal,
The endless games and forts and make-believe in the
Bamboo house's lower level,
The talent shows,
The tennis house—the sprinkler, the old video TV,
and the tennis court games,
The Lighthouse meetings and breakfasts and baptisms,
The horses and feeding them carrots
from the back of the truck,
The relays and Ragnars and more recently
The games on Grandchildren's green,
The marvelous Grammie Camps at the Lighthouse,
The motor home trips.

Bonding with cousins
And realizing that they fall somewhere between
siblings and friends
On the importance scale;
Cousins for life, Groups forever,
And you three, as the Old Faithfuls,
Stand atop the pyramid as the leaders and the
Example setters for all the rest
And another memory, a multifaceted one,
Of the Grandfather's Secrets—
Hearing them, discussing them, memorizing them,
Applying them to life.
Hiking up to Singletree, laughing
about good and bad popularity,
Feeling the Joy of Joy and the Spirit of
Sharing.

This email today is to introduce the last secret, number 10, and discuss how it can change your life.

But let me say first that just thinking about the secrets brings with it visions of the places we talked about them—the aqua blue lake, the sand, the tennis court, the big house, the pavilion, the lighthouse, the sailboat, and in the car on the way to Dingle or to the Bear Cave. I can see in my mind each of your faces and hear your voices as you came to understand each secret and realize why it was important.

So before we get to number 10, let's take a minute and think of the whole list. Can you remember where *you were when you first learned each of them? Can you remember how you thought about it and of situations you had been in or friends where it would apply? Can you remember when you taught and tutored younger cousins on what each secret meant and helped them on their memorizing?*

I love each of these secrets. I love them even more because they have become part of the bond between us. I know they are true principles and that they each connect to happiness and to a life well lived.

All of you know numbers 1 through 9, and this email will introduce and explain number 10, so that we can really talk about it this summer.

1. *LEADING: "Most kids are waiting for someone to lead them, but they just don't know it yet."*

2. *POPULARITY: "Good popularity comes from being nice to everyone, and it lasts. Bad popularity comes from only being nice to certain people, and it doesn't."*

3. *JOY: "Joy is the purpose of life and a choice you make."*

4. *COUSINS: "Blood is thicker than water, and cousins are more important than friends. We will stay close to each other and set a good example for each other and be there for each other."*

5. *CHOICES: "Prayer can help you on all of your choices, large and small."*

6. *SINGLE TREE: "You are unique, and there is only one of you. Find your place and grow into all you can be. Seek a life of Broadening and Contributing."*

7. *CHRIST: "In the great drama of life, Jesus Christ plays all of the leading roles, including Creator, God, Savior, Light, and Judge. Any family or individual who centers their testimony and life on Christ cannot fail."*

8. *TRANSFORMER: "Sex, between eternally married partners, is the most bright and beautiful and miraculous thing in this world. Any other uses of sex can darken the light. Sexual feelings are a gift from God and can always be transformed from dark to light."*

9. *MONEY AND MEANS: "Money is a 'means' and not an 'end;' a tool to be used, not a status to be gained. Too little or too much enslaves, while the enough-range liberates. '10-20-70' ensures 'enough and to spare.'"*

Now let's get into the big number 10 . . .

Why is this one the most important secret to you at this stage of life?

Of all the secrets, it is number 10 that may be the biggest factor in your lives right now and over the next few years. In the next five to ten years, you will likely make the most important decisions of your entire lives. In a way, it is unfair—maybe you would like to live a little longer and get a little wiser before making the biggest choices of all; but now, while still teens or in the early twenties, you will decide on college, on missions, on career (at least, initially), on marriage, and on family. You will wish, at times, that you could put these "biggies" off or that they didn't come at you quite so fast, and they will scare you! They should scare you, because they are so important and so big. They scare you because you realize that you will only make most of those decisions once, and that what you choose will change and determine the rest of your life.

But I believe that God does not leave us to make them on our own. He is there. His Spirit is willing and able to help. Let's read number 10:

10. DECISIONS: "In the second seventh of life come life's pivotal decisions, which will largely determine the happiness of the remaining five sevenths. Binary, right-wrong choices should be made in advance, dated and signed in contract with self. Open-ended, multi-alternative, confirmation-requiring decisions should be made tentatively through analysis, advice, and prayer, but not implemented or acted upon until they are verified by a Spiritual Process called 'confirmation.'"

Here is the reason I say you will make most of the big decisions in the "second seventh" of your lives: You and your generation, if you take care of yourselves and *live the rules of health, and if you are blessed to avoid serious accident or mortal illness, can expect to live for at least ninety years. If we assume ninety-one years, we can divide that number into seven periods of thirteen years each.*

In your first seventh, you were a child—a kid growing up—learning a ton and developing the foundation for what you are now. You became a teenager at the end of your first seventh, and lots of things started to change. Your hormones made their presence known, and you were sometimes happy or sad for no apparent reason. Friends got even more important to you and you began to think about new things—like the opposite sex.

Then, you entered the second seventh—the critically important years between 14 and 27—the time when you grow into your body, when you develop your uniqueness and your identity, when you leave home for the first time, and when you make the most important choices of your life.

Now, you may say to yourselves, how can Grandfather even remember the second seventh? He is so OLD! Well, let me tell you, I remember it very clearly, and I have seen each of my nine kids go through that second seventh, too—your moms and dads—so I am actually quite an expert on it, and I'm going to tell you in this little mini-book the secrets to making it work for you!

BINARY DECISIONS–THE FIRST TYPE OF CHOICES WE MAKE A LOT OF IN THE SECOND SEVENTH

The fact is, there are two very separate KINDS of decisions you have or will make during this second seventh. The first kind should be the easiest, but it isn't always so. The first kind is on the two-alternative, right-wrong kind, which you should be able to make IN ADVANCE. We are talking about decisions like whether you will ride in a car where the driver has been drinking, whether or not you will ever experiment with drinking or smoking or drugs, whether or not you will look at porn, whether or not you will be honest, whether or not you will apply yourself and do your very best at school, whether or not you will remember and follow the GF secrets, whether or not you will be kind and treat everyone equally, whether or not you will pay a full tithe and attend all church meetings and accept all church assignments.

These kinds of decisions should be the easiest, because they are really all the same decision: whether or not you will follow God's commandments. (I like to think of commandments as "loving council from a wise Father.") I like to call this first type of decisions "Binary Decisions," because there are only two possible answers, and one is right and the other is wrong.

You have already made a list of "decisions in advance" (see chapter 1) in your journal, and I think you dated them and signed them. You should refer to these often and re-commit yourself to them as you get older and as some of them become a bit harder.

OPEN-ENDED DECISIONS (OEDs)—THE SECOND KIND OF BIGGIES THAT COME DURING THE SECOND SEVENTH

The second kind of decisions that come at you during this second seventh can be a bit more complicated. They are the ones with multiple, often unknown alternatives that cannot be made in advance because we don't fully know exactly what the decision is or what it will involve or even exactly when it will happen. These are the decisions like who to marry, where to live, what to major in and graduate in from college, when to have a child, how many children to have, whether to go on a mission, what job to take and what career to pursue, and so on.

I like to call these the "Open-Ended Decisions" or OEDs because we don't even know what they all are yet or what or how many options we may have.

With these OEDs, there is a way to get "confirmation" that we have made the right or the best choice before we go ahead. It is kind of like a formula, and if we follow it, we will never have to second-guess or wonder if we made the right decision.

That formula is: Analysis of options + thoughtful, prayerful consideration + tentative decision + asking God if the decision we made is right = confirmation (sureness and commitment.) Let me explain:

The whole thing is based on something I know to be true. If we take this approach—coming to our decision carefully and prayerfully—and then we take that decision to God in prayer, one of two things will happen when we ask God if we have made the right choice: Either we will have a calm, sure, spiritual confirmation, a peaceful assurance that what we have decided is right; OR we will have a confused feeling, essentially the opposite of a confirmation—an uncertain, vague feeling that tells us we have to go back and think it through again and start over on the confirmation process.

When you think about it, this is a huge blessing. We can actually have God tell us, absolutely, if the tentative decision we have made is right. We can avoid making a big, wrong decision that will affect our life negatively, and we can be assured that once we have the confirmation, we are on the right path and doing the best thing. What a blessing! Because if we make the wrong choice about marriage or career or having a child or so many other things, it can contribute to unhappiness forever.

A Story to Illustrate

Let me tell you a story I've mentioned to you before that made it clear to me how this all works:

In college, I had met the beautiful Linda and fallen head over tails in love! But I was SO scared! How could

I make a decision this big? How could I decide something that was forever? How did I know enough to know if this was the ONE!?

I got so scared and bugged and crazy that I didn't know what to do. Actually, I was just totally lovesick. I couldn't concentrate in school, I couldn't focus on anything, all I could think about was HER, and I really was just kind of paralyzed about what to do.

Then, I remembered that I had a mentor, a wonderful older man who had given me good advice before. Impulsively, I got in my car early one morning and drove two hours to his office. I got there before the building was open and waited on the front steps. When a guard opened the building, I went up to my mentor's office and told his secretary that I NEEDED to see him. She was a very cold, official woman, and I remember she said, "Well, so do a lot of people—do you have an appointment?" I sort of stammered, "No, but you don't understand, I NEED to see him." Looking a little peeved, but I think worried that I might be suicidal, she said, "Wait here," and went into his office.

She came out and said, "He has an appointment with someone who is running late, so you can go in for a few minutes." I scrambled in, all nervous and weird, but my kind, old mentor just said, "Sit down, Richard. What can I help you with?" I stammered something like, "Well, I need to know if I should get married!"

He kind of smiled and said, "That's easy. You should!" And I said, "No, what I mean is, should I marry Linda?"

"Well," he said, having a little fun with me, though I didn't realize it at the time, "Tell me a little bit about this Linda of yours."

I started telling him all these great things about Linda, and he listened with an amused little smile on his face, and then I asked, "But how am I to know if I should marry her?" He asked me if I had thought about it and prayed about it and I said, "It's all I think about, and I've even asked God, and He won't tell me what to do!"

Then, he taught me this great lesson that I am now teaching you. He said, "I've always found on big decisions that you have to do the hard, analytical work and make your own best choice—and then God will tell you if you are right or not."

Then he did an amazing thing. He stood up and came around the desk and put his arm around me and said, "Look, it's obvious that you are in love and that you want to marry this girl, but just to be sure it is right, make a formal decision in your mind, and then, try fasting. Go without food for a day and then, go somewhere up in the mountains and ask God if your choice to marry Linda is the right one and if it is in line with His will."

This summer, when I see you, I'll tell you in person the story of my twenty-four-hour fast and the *confirmation I received while kneeling in the snow up in a canyon, but for now, let me just say that on that snowy day, when I told God that I loved Linda and had made my own decision to ask her to marry me and asked if He would please confirm that my decision was right, I received a calm, powerful witness that it was absolutely right in God's sight—I knew it so certainly and so surely that I have never doubted it, and that confirmation has been one of the greatest blessings of my life. And I proposed to your Grandma the next week! (Luckily, she got the same confirmation.)*

So, like I said, I will tell you more about that whole experience some day when we are together at the Lake. But for now, just focus on the process!

1. *Think hard, study it out, analyze, list pros and cons, pray for a clear mind and inspiration, and come to the best decision you can.*

2. *Take that decision to God and you are promised either a calm confirmation or a confused stupor. If you get the confirmation, do it! If not, go back and start over on your thought and study.*

It's not just the huge OED decisions like college or major or marriage or career that this formula works on. You great and wonderful grandkids are also making decisions right now that could have big consequences—deciding which classes to take, deciding whether or not to go out for a sport or try out or run for a position or an office, deciding on whether to apply for a job or a position . . . anything like this is an OED and the two step formula WORKS every time.

And don't forget the other kind of decisions, the binary ones that happen all the time. If you have decided in advance to look for kids who are lonely, to be friendly and kind even when you don't feel like it, or to not go along with friends when they are doing something that doesn't feel right; when you have thought these things through and written them down on your list of decisions in advance, you are stronger for it, more relaxed, and more confident.

More than anything, I want you to make the Binary Decisions in advance and to make the OEDs by the two-step formula. If you do, I promise you that you will make the right (and the best and happiest) choice for you on every important thing in your life.

I love you,
GF

Summary and Guidelines

If you had a magic wand and could wave it over your grandchildren and automatically imbue them with certain truths and guidelines for life, what principles would you implant in them? What are the things you have learned and that you wish you had learned earlier? Put some thought into this and follow this sequence:

» *Sit down and think about the principles you want to teach your grandkids.* This is some hard, mental work, and you won't complete your list in one sitting or in just a week or two. Think about it for at least a month, letting your thinking develop and evolve, and when you are ready, make a list of the principles you most want your grandkids to know. Try for between five and ten principles.

» *Think about how to state those principles simply and as "secrets."* Take another month, and gradually work each of your principles into a clear, terse sentence or two that a child can memorize and remember.

» *Tell your grandchild or grandchildren that you have some secrets for them* and that you will tell them just one of the secrets each year. Start the secrets with any grandchild who is eight or older. Make a big deal out of sharing each secret—do it in a special, one-on-one setting with the grandchild (or with two or three if you have some that are roughly the same age).

One way of thinking about this is that you don't want your dear and precious grandchildren to have to rediscover the wheel—or to learn hard lessons only by trial and error or by getting knocked down and beat up because they didn't know any better. Making a deliberate effort to teach your grandkids the life principles you think are most important is both a responsibility and an honor.

BEING A GATHERER

ONE WHO BRINGS EVERYONE TOGETHER FOR
REUNIONS, CREATING FUN TIMES, BONDING,
LOYALTY, AND LASTING FRIENDSHIPS
BETWEEN COUSINS

It's a Growing Organization Now, and You Are the CEO

Your individual relationships with each of your children and each of your grandchildren is forever important and can be the source of teaching, of unique loving, and of joy. But, besides the individual time, there should be collective time—places and time-spans where families bond, where cousins become almost like siblings, where everyone catches up on everyone else, and where a kind of family love and solidarity re-stokes and replenishes itself on a regular basis.

One of the most exciting things about the autumn of life is that your family begins to grow geometrically. Instead of the single option of one-at-a-time births in nuclear families, you now have marriages, and babies being born to the new households of your children, and perhaps your nieces and nephews.

You shift gears, and additional children come along via the marriages of our children, and in the form of additional cousins and great-nieces and great-nephews, and on and on it goes. And whether the numbers are large or small, there are different branches on the tree and on the neighboring trees that share the same root structure.

As we begin to truly understand that blood is thicker than water, we begin to feel the need to create a meaningful form of larger, extended family organization, communication, and management. In today's nomadic, fast-changing world, it takes conscious and deliberate effort to keep families together, in touch, and in sync, and grandfathers are the best candidates for that job. Whether we are talking just about our children, their spouses, and our grandchildren, or whether we are talking about the bigger picture of cousins, our own parents, and even "co-grandparents" (which is what I like to call the parents of those who have married my children and with whom I share or will share the same grandchildren), making it all work as a cohesive and somewhat unified family will take some real effort and some careful thought. And while every family is different, there are certain approaches that seem to always work.

Solidifying Relationships through Family Gatherings

Whether you live on the same street or your kids are far-flung; and whether you have one child or five, it is so important for your children and grandchildren to have bonding experiences that create lasting memories. Unless you are proactive about these get-togethers, whether formal or informal, it is so easy for families to drift apart and become disconnected.

Everyone's plan will be different depending on numbers and distances involved, as well as on financial issues, but there are four things that ought to be a part of everyone's "family gathering plan."

The four are:

1. *Place*: Having a traditional place or location to gather.

2. *Family Reunions*: Structuring and organizing our gatherings and making them happen regularly, so that they help each family member grow and progress.

3. *Specialized Retreats*: Dads forming fun getaways with sons and sons-in-law, as well as other "specialized" family groups—single kids, in-laws only, your children without grandchildren, and so on.

4. *Generation One and Generation Three Plans*: Well-conceived plans that bring you into focused, purposeful, memorable contact with your grandkids.

Let's take a little deeper look at each of the four:

PLACE: A TRADITIONAL LOCATION TO GATHER

Our gathering place, as you know by now, happens to be a little compound we have built gradually over the years at Bear Lake, a natural aqua-blue gem in the mountains on the border of Utah and Idaho. We've been spending family time at this lake for thirty-five summers. More communication, more relaxing, more sharing, and more *fun* seems to happen there in the few days or weeks we spend together each year than in all the rest of the time and all the rest of the places put together.

Families with grown-and-departed children need a *place* to gather and to communicate. It ought to be a place somewhat removed from the daily routine and from the normal distractions of work, friends, and commitments. Days seem so much longer at a place like this—there is more time to talk and to listen and to enjoy each other. There also seems to be more time and more opportunities to discuss problems or choices and to help each other with solutions and decisions.

For some, this place might just be the family home to which kids return. But the problem there, usually, even if you have room, is that most of us have a busy work life and social life revolving around our home, so we are not really getting away when the kids visit. A *second* place—somewhere else to go—where the dynamics and perspectives change a little—is worth its weight in gold.

And, by the way, it doesn't have to cost very *much* gold. One family we know just uses their old Winnebago. Once they're all crammed into it together, they start to talk and have fun on a different level. Another family has a very inexpensive vacation rental that they go to in the off-season. Friends in Bulgaria and the Ukraine, though they earn virtually nothing by American standards, still have a little "dacha"—a tiny country or forest cabin, often that they built themselves, where they can get away as a family. Still other families simply go camping to some familiar place they have come to know and love.

In our own case, we started with a rough little one-room-and-loft, A-frame at Bear Lake. It was all we could afford, but it was a place to start making memories as a family. It has grown and been added onto over the years, and now, whenever we want to get together for real talking and real fun, it generally happens at Bear Lake. In recent years, our grandchildren are forming some of the same memories that our children have from this place. This is where so many of our traditions happen, and while we're glad we started coming here when our kids were small, if we hadn't done it before, we'd do it now—for our grown family. We would invest in a place to gather and to enjoy and to re-bond.

Not that there aren't other options and methods for gathering. My brother creates the same sort of bonding in a different place each year. He'd rather rent than own— just for the flexibility and variety, and to avoid having another place to take care of, pay taxes on, and worry about. Many families we know find that their best bonding comes while camping together. Others, particularly those who have family "issues" with some of their siblings or in-laws, start with something shorter and on neutral territory—something as simple as a nice dinner together.

If none of these is an option for you because of distance and expense, luckily there are ways to have a family reunion of sorts online with Skype or Google Plus and other websites that can accommodate up to ten lines communicating in a virtual meeting on their computers.

Reunions

There are so many ways to have a successful family reunion. Since we are many years into it, we have some specific things that have become important to us during our reunions. You may want to grab some of these ideas for your own reunions and add your own tried-and-true formulas. We hope the following thoughts are a catalyst to start thinking about what you can do to be more effective in getting your family together regularly. In our case, although we see our family members often during the year, this is usually our only time to be *all* together.

It seems that there are also four indispensable ingredients in a successful family reunion. We call them the 4 Fs:

1. Facilitation (having one of your grown kids in charge and everyone involved)
2. Food (which not only attracts everyone, but stimulates conversation)
3. Fun (because this is the real point, right?)
4. Forum (because the other purpose is communication and resolution)

FACILITATION

The goal here is to have everyone feel included and to avoid too much of the responsibility falling to any one or two people (particularly to you!).

» Have your grown kids organize the reunion. After killing ourselves to create what we thought would be fun components of a great family reunion for several years, we decided that it was time to turn it over to the kids. They agreed (partly, because they all thought I planned too many meetings when I was in charge). The kids now rotate by couples, oldest to youngest, to organize our time together each year, and the designated couple is completely in charge. We've found that the less *you* (the grandparents) do, the better.

» Decide on a reasonable amount of time to be
together. Working with the schedules of all of our
children and the vacation allowances of their jobs
(and those pesky in-laws who annoyingly insist on
time with their kids, too) we can usually only eke
out four or five days for our "official" reunion each
summer. It is usually Wednesday night to Sunday
afternoon the first full week in July. Fortunately,
many of the moms and kids can stay on for a couple
of weeks before or after the reunion, and the working dads and moms try to get back on weekends.

» Assign grandchildren responsibilities. The larger the
group, the more important this becomes. The chaos
of having lots of people in relatively close quarters
and eating out of the same kitchen three meals a day
becomes pretty overwhelming. As our grandchildren got older, we realized that they felt ownership
in the reunion by being assigned to keep things
clean and orderly. The reunion organizers provide
a "chore chart" for the grandchildren. Each one is
assigned a task like loading the dishwasher, empty-
ing the dishwasher, sweeping the floor, clearing the
tables, vacuuming, and keeping the bathrooms clean
and stocked with toilet paper and towels. There are
points given for completing the tasks. Those with
the most points get a really fun prize like sleeping
over on the sailboat or the tennis court or a trip to
our favorite hamburger stand. The competition to
win can be intense!

FOOD

Providing food for several families, three meals a day for four days, is no small feat. From our Bear Lake spot, it is a one-hour round trip to the nearest grocery store, so we literally bring the food in by the truckload! It is never simple, but here are some things that have made it doable:

- » Menus and Responsibility: Each family is in charge of a meal, and since most have to fly to get there, the family in charge sends Linda and me the list of ingredients they need. If we can get it at Costco, we are happy to gather it up. If special ingredients are needed at a grocery store or a special market, they are in charge of getting it there.
- » We love trying new things each year. We have several gourmet cooks in the family, and we are provided delicious, beautiful, and unique meals. Recipes are shared, and we eat well!
- » Although we used to organize all three meals each day, we have decided to let each family fend for themselves for breakfast. If someone wants to flip some pancakes or make a big pot of oatmeal, then that is totally up to them.
- » Paying for the food is always an issue. Linda and I have decided to save up during the year and pay for the reunion food ourselves just to make it easier for the families traveling in. Other families we know, including those of some of our in-laws, divide up the cost of the food and the accommodations, and

share the cost equally. There are a lot of determining factors in this formula, and each family needs to come up with their own way.

FUN

Here are some ideas that we've tried. We've added to the list as the years have gone by and different kids have come up with fun new things to try. You'll want to adjust to your own activities according to numbers and ages.

- » In recent years, two of our technical wizards have helped us do a music video. They send out a song and have each member of the family lip-sync or dance to the rhythm for a few seconds on the video. The result is actually pretty amazing. To view them, go to youtube.com/eyresontheroad.
- » When we gather each summer at Bear Lake, water-skiing is a top priority. When the wind is calm and the water becomes a sheet of glass, we drop whatever else we're doing and head for the boat. Now that we are getting older, we've added a sailboat for those who like the quieter and calmer side of fun.
- » About a month before the reunion, the organizers ask everyone, including the kids (with the help of their parents) to email their favorite song of the year to the reunion chairman. Our techie kids have figured out how to put them all in an MP3 file and play the songs on the beach around a campfire as everyone guesses whose favorite song it is. Last year, we

added glow sticks to the mix. Everyone was given a glow stick, and when their song was played, they got to light their glow stick. It was a beautiful sight to see those glow sticks bouncing at the end of the evening as a spontaneous dance party broke out on the beach, making it a night to remember.

» Because we are tennis nuts and have a court at the lake, our reunions also include the annual Eyrealm (those who are in the realm of Eyres) Mixed Doubles Tennis Tournament. (Everyone who is married must partner with his or her spouse, which is entertaining in and of itself.)

» The past couple of years, we've had what we call the Bear Lake Family Ragnar. This has evolved because several of our kids are runners, and we now have a group big enough for every member to participate in the race. Each team has a car, and each runner has a team-coded color and number. Everyone who can walk, right down to the eighteen-month-olds, tag-team run the eleven miles to the nearest raspberry shake stand. To *most*, it is not about winning, but about having fun (we do have a couple of type-A competitors who want to win by hook or by crook who keep us all laughing). Last year, we were assigned to take pictures with our team at designated places along the route to prove we had run the entire course. And those raspberry shakes taste so good at the end of our raucous race!

» Our own take on the TV game "Fear Factor" has provided endless entertainment and may even be helping our kids be brave enough to try new things. The grandkids have a love-hate relationship with this game. "Wild and scary" food from all over the world (thanks largely to our son who spent two years in Japan) is given in small doses and over several "rounds" to our contestant grandkids. When they are shown the fabulous prizes (most from the dollar store) that go to those who complete each round, they are ecstatic. Each child who "just can't eat it" drops out after that round and is given a prize for trying. The prizes get better and better as the food gets harder and harder to eat. The parents and the kids who have already dropped out are watching the hysterical expressions on the kids' faces as they try their best to pretend they like seaweed or boiled squid. We learn pretty quickly which grandchildren are more adventuresome and which foods some kids simply cannot eat (e.g., quail eggs). Sometimes, the most timid kids from one year end up winning the contest the next year. Last year, our pickiest eater won the whole thing. Go figure!

» Late-night marathons of "Speed Scrabble," "Reverse Charades," and "Scum" (a hard-to-explain card game) provide lots of laughs and entertainment.

» We have also had fun with swimming races, gunny-sack races, relay races, rock-skipping contests, and a few more exotic things like the cow-pie toss and the sagebrush slalom.

FORUMS

In among the fun and the food, there will be some time for family meetings. Take time to hear from each family on their "happys" and "sads" over the past year. Discuss family history and tell some ancestor stories. Talk about the best movies you have seen and the best books you have read. Consider having a reunion theme that represents a positive change you all agree to work on together during the coming year.

F&FFE and Other Adult Gatherings

I bless the day that I started F&FFE (Fathers and Future Fathers of Eyrealm).

The bonding, brother to brother, brother-in-law to brother-in-law, and brother to brother-in-law—not to mention son or son-in-law to me—is extraordinary.

We find a long weekend and spend it together. If there is long-distance travel involved, we have a travel fund to which we each contribute what we can. We've gone scuba diving in Mexico, we've trekked to the bottom of the Grand Canyon, we've backpacked through Zion National Park on horseback, and we've gone to tennis tournaments together.

And, in there among the fun, we occasionally find a moment or two to talk about fathering and families.

It's also great to occasionally plan a separate getaway with all your adult children and their spouses without the kids. We had done that with a spur-of-the-moment dinner or movie when we were visiting our kids, but we wanted a real getaway, something planned a year in advance to a fun place that was affordable and exciting.

The first chance came when we sold our family home. This is a house that we had used for a home base for thirty-five years, and our children were not happy about giving it up, even though they had not been living there with us for some time! "You can't sell our home, the place where we spent so much of our lives and that holds so many wonderful memories," they said. "I want to bring my children home to see the room I grew up in and to meet the neighbors that I loved!"

Well, to make a long story short, we sold it! But we did get a good idea about how to soften the blow. In our travels throughout the world, we have to say that our favorite place on the earth is Bali, a magical, mystical island of Indonesia in the Indian Ocean that we had visited several times and fallen in love with. (In fact, we had sent two containers full of furniture, old ironwood beams, and carvings from Bali that we had used to create our new "downsized" home.)

So, we called the kids one-by-one and told them that we had bad news and good news: The bad news was that we had sold the house. The good news was that we were going to take them and their spouses to Bali with some of the profit from the house! In a split second, they made an about-face. They were delighted! They realized that a photo album detailing all the rooms and things in that old house that they were attached to would work just fine for their future memories!

We planned the trip a year in advance. It was so fun to look forward to and anticipate it together. And it was even more fun as we planned the incredible logistics behind getting everybody there. We won't bore you with the details, but we have to say that more bonding went on among our kids (without their kids) during that week than we could have accomplished in any other way.

While most will not take their grown children and their spouses to Bali, some kind of adult-only gathering is worth what it takes to make it happen. Even in cases where adult children may not be on the best of terms, doing something really fun together may soothe some sore feelings and have a surprisingly positive effect.

One sidenote on downsizing: When we sold our house, the conundrum was who should get the furniture? All of our kids wanted the same pieces. So we held an auction. We gave each of our children $40,000 of play money, put bidding numbers on each piece of furniture, and hired a real auctioneer with a fast voice, a top hat, and a gavel. Two of our children who couldn't get to the auction were on Skype and bidding by phone. They were all able to bid for what they wanted, and we escaped without having to make any arbitrary decisions or show any favoritism.

OTHER WAYS TO HAVE FAMILY GATHERINGS

There are many different kinds of family gatherings. One alternative is to do a service project or some kind of humanitarian project together. We have had life-changing experiences in Bolivia, Africa, Mexico, and India with as many of our children and grandchildren as could go.

It wasn't long before we discovered that we could go on one of these expeditions for less cost than a vacation at Disney World and/or some other typical vacation. We also found that the service element of these trips enhanced our internal family interaction, bonding, and communication.

We have also realized that you don't have to go to a third-world country to derive these benefits of service. A full-family "mini-expedition" to feed the homeless at a shelter provides the same kind of bonding and communication and the same kind of perspective and gratitude boost. It is a fantastic trip for a grandfather to take with his grandkids.

Summary and Guidelines

I actually like the word and the idea of "institutionalizing" a family—meaning to make it strong, lasting, and cohesive with the history and the traditions that hold its members close and that give everyone a larger-than-self identity. A brief review of some of the things you can do to bring this about:

- » *Be the CEO and the organizer.* In this world of movement and change, it's not easy to keep a family together. Years can slip by, and people, even siblings and cousins within families, can lose touch and grow apart. With deliberate effort and strategy, though, you can keep your family close and in touch despite distance and separate lives.
- » *Orchestrate reunions.* Nothing is better than all being together—regularly. Find a permanent place or pattern and make them happen. Have an agenda, have a plan, and do it every year!
- » *Find other ways to gather key parts of the family.* Do some things with adults only—your kids and

spouses. Plan some things just with your son(s) and son(s)-in-law, and other things with your daughter(s) and daughter(s)-in-law. And, of course, sometimes just with your grandkids. It all takes time, but it's all worth it. Relationships are more important than achievements, and relationships with your family, every part of your family, are the most important thing of all.

Most of us have a bit of social organizing and conferencing in our DNA, and what better place to apply it than in our families. Like it or not, you are the patriarch, and if you don't do it, who will?

BEING A FINANCIAL FACILITATOR

ONE WHO PROVIDES THE MATCHING GRANTS,
LOANS, AND EQUITY THAT CAN FUEL GRANDKIDS'
INITIATIVE AND HELP THEM MOVE FORWARD
FASTER TOWARD THEIR GOALS

When Grandkids Seek Their Own Orbit

This chapter can be thought of as a kind of follow up or part two to chapter 6 on being an Independence-Giver. Let's say you have done what you can to help your grandkids begin the progression toward being independent and self-determining. Now, the question comes, "How can I facilitate the fulfillment and flowering of that independence as they leave their parents' homes and move into their separate lives?"

Clearly, if you have a spouse, this question is one for the two of you to discuss and resolve together, in concert with your best legal advisor, and, of course, in communication and in sync with your kids. Think of this chapter as a few ideas and inputs to that process.

Now, without being morbid, let's acknowledge that there are really two parts to this question about helping grandkids financially: 1. What can I do while I'm alive? and 2. What can I do after I'm dead?

And actually, let's take the second one first.

A Matching Educational Trust Fund

One thing most of us know is that we would like to help in any way we can with our grandchildren's education; and one thing very few of us know is when we will not be around to help anymore. So, if you have the means, it makes sense to set up some kind of an educational trust fund.

If you do, the following guidelines are suggested:

» Set it up with an attorney and estate planner that you trust. But don't count on him or her to decide or dictate your objectives. You figure out exactly *what* you want the trust to accomplish and let the pros help you with the *how*.

» A matching provision. Make it so that your funds match, one to one, the funds that they can come up with themselves, either with their own savings, their parents' contribution, or scholarships and loans (or any combination of the three). Without entitling or undermining independence, this allows a grandchild to attend a school twice as expensive as he or she could otherwise afford; or to go sooner and finish earlier than he or she otherwise could.

» Have it be for education generally, not university specifically. A trade school or apprenticeship should be as honored and supported as an Ivy League college.

» Set it up in such a way that there is an equal amount available for each grandchild.

» Have provisions that take the full amount you have allocated in your will and divide it equally among your grandkids at the time of your death or your wife's death, if that comes later; and make each share available as a post–high school education matching fund. Decide if you want it to go only toward tuition or to apply as a match to all education expenses, including room and board.

» If a grandchild decides not to pursue post–high school education, his or her share is evenly divided among the other grandchildren's shares. The same happens with any leftover funds (amounts in a grandchild's share that were not matched and used).

What about Education Expense Help While You Are Alive?

The reason we talked about the "dead" option first is that the live option ought to follow similar guidelines. The difference is that while you are still here and in control, you can tailor your matching and supplementing gifts to individual needs, and combine it with the consulting principles from chapter 6.

While you are alive, you may have one grandchild whose parents have done very well and who doesn't need any financial help for university; and you may have another grandchild whose parents can't help much at all. You can step in to fill the void. But the best way is not with an outright, entitling gift. Instead, you want to structure your help in a way that gives the child real ownership of her education, and the independent and fulfilling feeling that she has paid for her own college tuition and expenses.

This can be done by discussing a matching agreement with your grandchild and his or her parents. The two simple guidelines might be:

1. I will match the funds you can come up with 1:1 (one dollar from me for each dollar from you) for all

of your college expenses (tuition, books, room and board).

2. This match will not be a gift, but a no-interest loan with a promissory note drawn up professionally and signed, but with no repayment requirement or schedule (you can repay it when you are able—to me or to the education trust).

Structuring it in this way has several advantages: First, the grandchild will have to be resourceful enough to come up with her half, whether it is from her own savings, her parents' contributions, or grants and loans from the college or the government.

Second, she will feel like it is totally her education because she is paying for it and will thus be more likely to do her best and maximize her academic achievement. And third, since there is no interest or repayment timetable on the grandfather's loan, she will be free to repay any other college loans and begin to build her own life and buy her own home and other things before she worries about repaying the loan from you.

Help on First Home Purchase

Another thing a lot of us would like to help with financially is the purchase of a first home for our children and our grandchildren. Oftentimes, kids just out of college and starting their careers have enough income to make monthly mortgage payments on a reasonable home but lack the liquidity to make the required down payment. In fact, many are paying a monthly rent amount that is as much as a mortgage payment would be if they were able to come up with the down payment necessary to buy a home. If parents can help with the down payment, they should be the first option, but you should be the second.

Generally, and historically, the buy option works out better financially than the rent option. For one thing, interest, which makes up most of the early monthly mortgage payments, is tax deductible; and second, well-chosen homes usually appreciate and become the primary investment of young people starting out.

Thus, if you are able to offer some financial help, covering a down payment can catapult a grandchild toward greater independence and larger net worth by allowing him to buy his or her first home.

A no-interest or low-interest loan similar to the education recommendations is one viable option, but a better and more educational one might be for you to simply take a small equity position in your grandchild's first home. This can be worked out rather simply and usually turns out to be a win-win.

For example, let's say you have a recently married and recently college graduated granddaughter who, with her husband, would like to buy a starter home; and say there is a 20 percent down payment required to get the best deal and to bring down the monthly mortgage payment to an amount they can afford—an amount roughly equal to the rent they are paying currently. The house is $250,000, so a $50,000 down payment is needed. The young couple has some savings but not nearly that much, and would like to keep their savings in a rainy-day fund rather than use it on the house.

You could agree (and a written agreement is essential) to make the down payment in return for a 20 percent equity position in the house and with the agreement that when the house is sold, you will receive 20 percent of the net selling price. If, in the meantime, the couple puts additional money into the home for improvement and fix-up, the basis will go up from $250,000 and your percentage of ownership will decline accordingly.

Let's say they buy the house with your down payment and take a mortgage loan with favorable interest for $200,000.

Your children benefit from all of the leverage on the house and will likely have the blessing of appreciation as well as the benefit of the interest write off while they keep the home.

Imagine that they keep and live in the home for five years before outgrowing it and choosing to move. And let's say that they have put an additional $28,000 into the home during the five years. The basis in the home is now $278,000, of which you paid $50,000, or roughly 18 percent. The house sells for $360,000, so your equity share is $64,800, and their share is $295,200, out of which they pay their remaining mortgage of about $180,000 and retain some $115,000 profit, which can go toward their next house. You made a reasonable return on your money, and they did much better, having turned their $48,000 ($20,000 principal paid over the five years plus $28,000 additional improvements) into $115,000 for a five-year gain of well over 100 hundred percent.

Setting Up a Family Foundation and Doing "Expeditions"

Every year during our summer family reunion, we hold the formal board meeting of the Eyrealm Foundation, a charitable trust we set up many years ago even though there was very little money in the trust initially. This annual meeting at the reunion is held after the grandkids are all in bed or downstairs watching a movie and is attended by our adult children and their spouses. We keep the meeting official with a secretary taking notes and formal votes to make decisions. Spouses attend and advise but don't have a vote. With our oldest daughter acting as the Chairwoman of the Board, our children decide what money should be allocated to selected 501(c)(3) nonprofit organizations that are helping with the needs of needy families and children.

We initially set up the foundation because we had the occasional nightmare that most parents do—of a lawyer's office where the kids, after your death, are fighting over your assets. We wanted to keep that visual dream of kids sitting around a boardroom table, but change the context so that, instead of fighting over inheritance, they are discussing how and to whom to give assets that have passed on not to them personally but to a charitable foundation of which they are the directors.

We had seen, for too long and in too many cases, how "inheritances" had messed up families, destroyed the incentive of children, and created intra-family conflicts and bitterness. We decided that our goal was to help our kids all we could, wisely, while we were alive and tell them all along that there would be no inheritance because we believed none of them would need it, and that our estate would go to a grand-children's education matching fund and to our charitable foundation.

The foundation's charter requires that funds go only to organizations that one of us has researched and become involved with personally. One son and his wife, who spent a one-year humanitarian honeymoon in Mozambique and India, ask for continuing funds to help with Care for Life, the organization they continue to work with in Mozambique. Some of our other children have been to Ethiopia, India, Bulgaria, and Mexico on humanitarian projects, some with us and some independently, and are invested in continuing support for these groups because they know and trust the vision and leadership of the organizations and understand the desperate needs of the recipients. Others of our children favor local soup kitchens and other closer-to-home needs. Our donations are not very large, but we have been able to help with some rather desperate situations. After we die, this organization will continue to be an important reason for the kids to get together, so they can decide where the funds should go; and the amounts available may be significantly larger because most of our estate, whatever is left after the provisions for the grandkids' education fund, will go to this family foundation.

The family foundation is a great way to bring the family together and focus on *charitable giving* rather than *selfish tak-ing*. Starting while you are still around and involved, you can help your kids learn the principle of "Where much is given, much is expected."

Summary and Guidelines

As your grandkids hit college age, you want to be able to help, but you hope to give that help intelligently so it benefits rather than undermines each of them. The key suggestions are:

» *Set up an educational trust fund in your will* that will provide matching funds for your grandkids' college or post-secondary education. Let your children and grandchildren in on the details of this fund so that they know both what to expect and what not to expect.

» *Explain carefully to family that the trust fund and other provisions in your will most likely will be a moot point* because you plan on living long enough to give the kind of educational assistance contemplated in your will, but to do so personally and based on need. Invite families and children to begin to think now about educational costs and to save and plan accordingly.

» *Offer to become an equity participant (by making the down payment) in your children's or your grandchildren's first home.* Have a clearly worded document that explains how the equity position works and how the profit percentages are split when the home is sold.

» *Consider setting up a Family Foundation*, with your children and older grandchildren as directors, to help less-fortunate families. Have a special meeting with your children and grandchildren in which the whole objective and purpose of the foundation is discussed and where you explain that, other than the grandchildren's educational trust, there will be no traditional inheritance upon your death; rather, all funds and assets beyond those earmarked for the educational trust will go into the foundation and your children will be the board that decides how and to whom those funds are given away.

Most of us grandfathers do not have vast resources with which we can assist our grandchildren at every turn or with every need. But whether we have a lot or a little, it is important to be deliberate and very clear in our own minds about what our goals are and how we can help our grandkids materially and financially in a way wise enough that it increases rather than diminishes their independence and sense of self-reliance.

■ GRANDPARENTING □
CHAPTER 10

BEING a
WORLD-OPENER

ONE WHO AWAKENS YOUR GRANDCHILDREN TO
THEIR OWN OPTIONS AND POTENTIAL AND TO THE
DIVERSITY AND OPPORTUNITY OF THE WORLD

Helping Your Grandkids to be Citizens of the World

Kids today have access to the whole world—on their screens and smartphones and on Google. But that virtual world is not the same as the real world, and sometimes grandparents can be the portal through which their grandchildren experience (and learn to think accurately and broadly about) the places and the breadth of the planet they actually live on.

You can be their oracle, in a way, not only through the stories you tell them, but through the things you show them and the places you actually take them.

Here are a couple of ideas that may spark other ideas:

Humanitarian Expeditions

It's fun—or at least parts of it are fun—to take a grandchild to an amusement park or a resort, but it is far more fun and vastly more beneficial to take that same grandchild to a part of the world that is way out of her comfort zone and that opens her eyes to the bigger world, particularly the Third World.

As mentioned briefly in chapter 8, there are numerous nonprofit organizations that orchestrate aid missions and humanitarian projects in various parts of the Third World and design these expeditions specifically for family participation. Many readers will be familiar with *Habitat for Humanity*, where families can go for a week or even a long weekend to build affordable housing for poor families in Mexico or other areas where there is high need for very basic shelter.

There are other nonprofits that set up one- or two-week projects of building a school, digging an irrigation system, organizing a health clinic, or providing micro-lending for new small business ideas—projects that families can participate in during the Christmas holidays or during school vacation periods in the spring or summer. Two of our favorite nonprofit organizations that are very good at organizing such expeditions are Rising Star Outreach, which builds and runs schools for leprosy-affected children in southern India, and Choice Humanitarian, which sets up water, educational, and agricultural projects in Mexico, Nepal, and other third-world locations.

To get beyond the "fake reality" of websites and video games and the not-much-better reality of the "global villages" of Disney World, we grandfathers, as our means allow, should look for opportunities to take our grandchildren out of their comfort zones and into the parts of the globe that they have never imagined and that they can never experience vicariously or in cyberspace or amusement park space.

Frankly, there is nothing quite like the experience and relationships provided by a situation with a grandfather and a couple of grandkids in a remote corner of the world without Wi-Fi or TV, giving real help and having genuine communication.

Funds from the type of family foundation discussed in the last chapter qualify for use in participating in all of these forms of humanitarian and charitable expeditions, although the experience will mean more to kids if they have earned part of the money it costs to go.

READING THROUGH THE MAJORS OFFERED AT UNIVERSITIES

It is remarkable how many kids start college these days with very little idea of what they want to study or what courses and majors would tie into their natural abilities and aptitudes. A surprising number of college freshmen and sophomores just pick a general studies major or study what their parent did or what a friend is majoring in, without any real or deliberate effort to know their options or to look for a match with their interests and abilities.

There are aptitude tests and orientation courses and other institutionalized methods for helping kids figure out their careers and decide on the emphasis and directions of their college or university training. But there is a much better source and method, and it is called grandfathers.

Pick up a course catalog from a good university (or find one online), and take your high school grandchild out for dinner some night. Turn to the list of degrees or majors and read through the entire list together and talk a bit about the ones he or she may not be familiar with. Have your grandchild rank each major with a 1, 2, 3, 4, or 5, depending on how interesting the major sounds with 1 being low interest and 5 being very high. Think together about what kind of career each major might lead to.

Discuss how the world is changing and how there are things to do in work and career and in educational focus that did not even exist a few years ago. Explain and discuss how important it is to think hard about what to study in college, and even to take some exploratory classes, various aptitude tests, and do a serious analysis of where his or her interests lie.

Traveling Together

It's not only third-world travel or humanitarian expeditions that expand kids' horizons and perspectives. Any kind of travel, particularly with a reasonably knowledgeable grandfather, can be a world-opener. Take your grandkids to places you love, whether those places are art galleries or hunting lodges. Share your passions geographically. One-on-one trips are usually best, although if you have a couple of grandkids roughly the same age, you can certainly take them together.

And play the other side of the interest coin also. Besides taking them to places that interest you and arouse your passions, find out what places might feed into your grandkids' current interests. This might tie naturally into your discussion of potential college majors. See which of their interests lend themselves to a particular place or experience, and try to find some places where a little grandfather-grandchild trip might be appropriate and fun.

Often, our time with grandkids is in little bursts—a quick visit, a meal together, a movie, or a little outing. These short-exposure events do not lend themselves to deep communication or gradually relaxing and rising trust levels. The inherent value of travel, particularly with just you and one or two grandkids, is that travel time is conversation and communication time, and the longer you are together, the more relaxed the atmosphere becomes and the more feelings and attitudes manifest themselves as trust develops.

Summary and Guidelines

Whoever you are and wherever you have been, as a grandfather, you are at one end of your life experience and your grandchildren are at the other end. You can and should seek to become one of your grandkids' primary and principal mentors as they grow and become acquainted with the world around them. Three possibilities:

1. *Awaken your grandchildren to the world by taking them into the world.* Simple little trips and visits to museums, factories, large cities, and small towns can be a kind of grandfather's field trip that will broaden the perspectives and open eyes of your grandkids.

2. *Do humanitarian expeditions with your grandkids.* The extreme version of "seeing the world" is seeing the Third World. Nothing increases a child's GQ (Gratitude Quotient) and CQ (Contribution Quotient) like spending a week or so of his or her school vacation or Christmas vacation living in a village in a developing country and giving service there while interacting with the children who live there.

3. *Help them think preliminarily about college by going through course catalogs.* Doing this and asking about and discussing strengths and weaknesses of various careers and getting into what aptitudes and interests are required for each can be a lot of fun, as well as

highly stimulating. Junior high is not too early to start this. The old "What do you want to be when you grow up?" question, which is fun at younger ages, can now start to be more in-depth and serious, and grandfathers can be great guides in the process.

Helping to raise a true "citizen of the world" should be one of our goals as grandfathers. We should use whatever resources we have to open doors of experience and perspective to grandkids, which will increase their capacity to contribute and open their eyes to the wonder and diversity of the world they live in.

SUMMING IT UP

I t's a whole new territory, this grandfathering—this GRANDfathering! It's a new field where not much has been written, and it's a new opportunity for far more men, now that we are living longer and having more freedom in our later years.

Not many of us want to make it (grandfathering) a full-time pursuit, but when we sit down and think about it, nothing in our lives is more delightful and more potentially rewarding than our relationships with our grandkids and the help we may be able to give them.

We've all learned, by this stage of our lives, that offense is a lot more fun than defense and that the way to approach opportunities and find fulfillment is to be proactive. Passive grandfathering—just paying a little attention once in a while or trying to lend a bit of financial support as needed—is not much fun.

The thing that often holds us back from greater involvement with our grandkids is that, in some ways, they lie a bit outside our comfort zones. We don't know exactly what they need or how to go about Proactive Grandfathering.

This book tries to be a bit of a guide, or at least an idea stimulator, because the more we think about grandfathering and the more we think about our grandkids, the more susceptible and open we become to ideas and to purposefully prioritizing these living legacies more than we have in the past.

There are more grandfathers in the world now than ever before. We are living longer and prioritizing better. All we need to prompt us into action is a few good ideas.

Two *don'ts* to keep in mind: (1) Don't try to do too much or implement too much of this book all at once. Better to pick two or three of the ideas that appeal to you and that you think your grandkids would respond well to, and to implement them; and (2) Don't let guilt or discouragement creep in as you read the many ideas and possibilities in this book. No one does it all—certainly not me. Think of this book as a philosophy for shifting into a more grandkid-centric lifestyle and as a grab bag of potential ideas to apply as you need them and as they appeal to you.

And as you strike out on this adventure, stay in touch. Our website is valuesparenting.com, and there is a "Contact Us" button there that goes directly to us. On *Valuesparenting*, you will find a bounty of good programs and ideas to refer your own kids to, and you will find greater expansion of and help with many of the suggestions found in this book.

Also, please find many of our books for free on EyreFreeBooks.com and get better acquainted with our family at Eyrealm.com.

Onward and upward!

RME, 2017

OTHER BOOKS BY RICHARD EYRE

Poems of Family and Favorites
The Half-Diet Diet
Tennis and Life
*Life in Full**
*The Turning**
*The Thankful Heart**
*On the Homefront**
*The Entitlement Trap**
*5 Spiritual Solutions for Everyday Parenting Challenges**
The Three Deceivers
Dr. Bridell's Rational Diet
*The Book of Nurturing**
*Empty-Nest Parenting**
*The Happy Family**
Life before Life
*How to Talk to Your Child About Sex**
*Spiritual Serendipity**
Spiritual Stewardship
The Wrappings and the Gifts
Don't Just Do Something, Sit There
*Three Steps to a Strong Family**
*Teaching Your Children Values**
Utah in the Year 2000
Stewardship of the Heart

Serendipity of the Spirit
More Children's Stories on Joy*
Lifebalance*
Teaching Your Children Sensitivity*
Teaching Children Charity*
12 Children's Stories on Joy*
Mother, Father, and the Family That Worked*
The Change That We Call Birth*
5 Children's Stories on Joy*
Free to be Free
Success Is . . .*
The Secret of the Sabbath
Teaching Your Children Responsibility*
Your Eternal Choice**
The Awakening
I Challenge You . . . I Promise You . . . Volume I**
I Challenge You . . . I Promise You . . . Volume II**
Simplified Husbandship, Simplified Fathership
Teaching Children Joy*
Life Planning
What Manner of Man
The Birth That We Call Death**
Goals**
The Discovery of Joy
Relationships: Self, Family, God**

*Coauthored with Linda

**Coauthored

About the Author

Richard Eyre and his wife, Linda, live and write in the mountains of Park City, Utah, when they are not on airplanes trying to keep up with their nine far-flung children and twenty-nine grandchildren.

About Familius

Visit Our Website: www.familius.com

Join Our Family

There are lots of ways to connect with us! Subscribe to our newsletters at www.familius.com to receive uplifting daily inspiration, essays from our Pater Familius, a free ebook every month, and the first word on special discounts and Familius news.

Get Bulk Discounts

If you feel a few friends and family might benefit from what you've read, let us know and we'll be happy to provide you with quantity discounts. Simply email us at orders@familius.com.

Connect

- » Facebook: www.facebook.com/paterfamilius
- » Twitter: @familiustalk, @paterfamilius1
- » Pinterest: www.pinterest.com/familius
- » Instagram: @familiustalk

The most important work you ever do will be within the walls of your own home.

CPSIA information can be obtained
at www.ICGtesting.com
Printed in the USA
LVOW12s0836070717

540500LV00001B/5/P